Internships in Recreation and Leisure Services

A Practical Guide for Students

Fifth Edition

Internships in Recreation and Leisure Services
A Practical Guide for Students
Fifth Edition

Edward E. Seagle, Jr., EdD
Tammy B. Smith, MS, PhDc
Ralph W. Smith, PhD

Venture Publishing, Inc.
State College, PA

Library of Congress Catalogue Card Number: 2012954990
ISBN-10: 1-892132-56-7
ISBN-13: 978-1-892132-56-7

Acknowledgments

The authors would like to thank the many people who helped to make this manual a reality, especially the faculty and students at California State University, Chico, and The Pennsylvania State University. The ideas, comments, contributions, and assistance of the following people deserve special recognition: James "Corky" Broughton, Murray State University; Steven Burr, The Pennsylvania State University; Judy Elliott, Lock Haven University; Robert Griffith, Pennsylvania Recreation and Parks Society; Frank Guadagnolo, The Pennsylvania State University; Deb Kerstetter, The Pennsylvania State University; Rod Warnick, University of Massachusetts; Tom Willson, formerly of Lock Haven University; and David Wood, formerly of the National Recreation and Park Association. The authors would also like to express sincere appreciation to the staff at Venture Publishing for the many hours of technical assistance they provided.

Aspects of the letters and résumés used in this text were modified from documents submitted by undergraduate students (now alumni) of California State University, Chico, and The Pennsylvania State University, and the authors gratefully acknowledge their assistance.

Ed Seagle extends his personal thanks to his wife, Sylvia Seagle; coworkers, students, and alumni at California State University, Chico; and his professional colleagues for their continued support. Thanks is also ex-tended to Buford Bush (Professor Emeritus) who appointed Dr. Seagle as Internship Coordinator at CSU, Chico, and the Recreation and Parks Management faculty members who have shown continued confidence in his performance as Internship Coordinator over the years. Dr. Seagle offers special thanks to Lola Dalton, who made substantial contributions to earlier editions of the book; Ken Steidley, Program Manager at Do-It Leisure, who has used the first edition of this book in internship preparation classes and has provided valuable feedback and suggestions for improvement; and Lisa Jorgensen, assistant professor at CSU, Sacramento. Another special thank you goes to Don Penland, Computer Director at CSU, Chico, for his review and editing of the computer-related information provided in this book.

In addition to The Pennsylvania State University faculty, Dr. Smith would also like to recognize the contributions of colleagues who assisted him during his years at the University of Maryland, particularly Viki Annand, Jimmy Calloway, the late Fred Humphrey, Seppo Iso-Ahola, and Veda Ward.

Contents

Introduction

Before anything else, preparation is the secret of success.—Alexander Graham Bell

You are approaching one of the most important academic decisions of your college years—selecting an internship site in recreation and leisure services. A good internship brings academic coursework to life and provides work experience and professional contacts that help to ensure a successful professional career. Your internship is the foundation for your future and like any strong foundation, its construction requires time, effort, and the proper tools. The purpose of this text is to give you the proper tools for getting the best possible internship—the time and effort, however, are up to you.

Before charging ahead, it is important to acknowledge some thoughts that many students have as they approach the internship search. These include:

- My GPA isn't very strong, so I probably won't be offered the best internships.
- I don't feel ready for entering the work environment…maybe I need to take more courses.
- I don't have a lot of work experience in recreation services. Why would an internship site want me?
- It's not what you know, but who you know that counts…and I don't know anybody!
- I don't even know where to start looking for an internship site.

Many college students are uncertain about their qualifications and career readiness, and most have some degree of anxiety about the future. Feelings of uncertainty and anxiety are normal, particularly when con-fronted with an important decision like internship selection. Hopefully, as you progress through this manual any uncertainties or anxieties you feel will fade and be replaced by the confidence that comes from doing a thorough job of preparation. Students who know the most people, have the best GPAs, or accumulate the most work experiences aren't necessarily the student selected by an internship site. Rather, internships are usually awarded to students who have taken the time to prepare, in detail, for their internship selection.

Without being aware of it, you have been preparing for your internship for years. People you have met, things you have done, and information you have collected throughout your life are all helpful in identifying and secur-ing an internship. In the chapters that follow, you will go through a systematic internship selection process that will help you utilize your life experiences and available resources to maximum advantage. The ultimate goal is to help you to identify and secure an internship that not only meets your academic objectives, but also enhances your professional career in recreation and leisure services. The internship selection process includes:

- Conducting a thorough self-assessment
- Determining your direction and setting internship goals
- Searching for appropriate agencies and researching the most promising ones
- Preparing to contact agencies, including writing cover letters and résumés
- Preparing for and participating in interviews
- Deciding which internship site is best for you

These steps parallel the employment-seeking process and are covered in detail in this manual. Each chapter (1) presents information for you to read and think about, (2) includes exercises for you to complete, and (3) lists, whenever appropriate, pertinent questions for you to ponder. The overall intent of the manual is to help you to develop effective internship tools and to refine your internship selection process. Throughout the manual, we have included examples from a variety of recreation and leisure service specializations (e.g., out-door recreation, therapeutic recreation, hospitality, special events, community recreation, commercial recreation, tourism) to il-lustrate important points and concepts.

As you read the chapters that follow, remember that your department's internship coordinator is a critical link in your internship selection process. Each college and university has its own procedures and policies related to internships in recreation and leisure services; therefore, prior to finalizing each step of the internship selection process outlined in this manual, you should consult with your internship coordinator and, if appropriate, your academic advisor.

Chapter One
Self-Assessment

Whether you believe you can do a thing or not, you are right.—Henry Ford

This chapter intends to assist you in identifying who you are and what you have to offer a potential internship agency. We will help you to examine your own self-confidence, personal philosophy, personality traits, professional skills, limitations, and attitude toward work. In doing this we hope to assist you in looking at your history/development and identifying those things that have helped you to become a unique human being. Examining yourself and your past is essential because *all* of your life experiences help to determine how you will approach your career choices. Self-exploration will help you to reach the internship and career goals you set. Knowledge is power, and an in-depth evaluation of yourself will provide the knowledge you need to assume power over your professional life.

In this chapter you will examine your own:
- Self-confidence
- Personal philosophy
- Interests and needs
- Personality traits and professional skills
- Limitations and weaknesses
- Attitudes toward work and learning

Self-Confidence

First, it is important to look at how you feel about your own abilities. If you believe in yourself, you are likely to have positive feelings about yourself *and* project a positive image to others. Since this is vital to your professional future, you need to take some time to assess your self-confidence. Specifically, you need to identify positive and negative statements (internal messages) that you make to yourself. It is especially important to note any negative statements and find ways to change them into positive ones.

Ask yourself the following questions. Each "yes" answer indicates that you are enhancing your own self-confidence and projecting a *positive* image to others. Do you:

- Regularly give yourself positive strokes for accomplishments?

  Examples include the following internal messages to yourself: *I did a good job preparing my résumé. When I made that presentation, I displayed confidence and spoke with authority. Way to go! I deserve congratulations on completing that assignment.*

- Use positive self-talk when you approach a challenge?

  Examples include: *I am confident in my abilities to perform this internship. I have what it takes to succeed in this internship. I have confidence in my interviewing skills. During this interview I will be on top, in control, and successful.*

- Use positive body language when interacting with others?

  Examples include: Displaying good sitting and standing posture, maintaining eye contact, using appropriate gestures to emphasize points.

- Use your voice effectively when communicating your thoughts?

  Examples include: Speaking in a clear and resonant voice, varying your inflection to maintain interest and emphasize important points, pronouncing words distinctly and with authority.

Now, ask yourself the following questions. Each "yes" answer may mean that you are doing things to undermine your own self-confidence and project a *negative* image to others. Do you:

- Regularly give yourself criticism for things you do or mistakes you make?

  Examples include the following internal messages to yourself: *There was not enough time to prepare a professional résumé. How could you be so stupid as to forget the answer to that question? There you go, messing things up again! You should have known better than to try that.*

- Use negative self-talk when you approach a challenge?

  Examples include: *I can't do this job. I'm not good enough to get selected for an interview. I did not get the last internship, so I will not get this one. I shouldn't even bother to try, it's too difficult for me.*

- Rationalize or minimize your successes?

  Examples include: *I don't deserve such a good internship. If it hadn't been for the help other people gave me, I never could have developed a decent résumé. Sure, I got the internship, but the competition wasn't very tough.*

Throughout the next week, analyze your own internal messages. Is your self-talk positive or negative? Do you give yourself credit for the good things that you do, or do you rationalize or minimize your accomplishments? If you find that you give negative messages to yourself, you need to work hard to change them. This can be done by:

- Being attuned to your self-talk
- Recognizing when a negative message is forming
- Interrupting, with positive thoughts, your own negative message *as soon as it starts*
- Consciously substituting positive self-talk in place of your negative message

Changing your self-talk is not easy. It is hard work, but it is well worth the effort. There are many examples of people who succeeded against difficult odds, and most of them did so because they would not allow negative self-talk to get in their way. By giving yourself positive messages, you will be able to maximize your abilities.

Personal Philosophy

A personal philosophy of life is something we all have, but many people have not thought about their own philosophy long enough to define it clearly. Understanding your personal philosophy is important because it gives you an advantage in an internship interview and guides your search for fulfilling employment in recreation and leisure services. A sound personal philosophy allows you to describe who you are and what life means to you. It also provides direction in your life by helping you recognize what things are important to you.

To examine your personal philosophy it helps to conduct a review of your life. How did you arrive at this point in your life? What life experiences have had a major impact upon your life? Who are the friends and relatives who have had an influence upon your life? What beliefs do you share with these individuals? What heroes have you had while growing up? What was it about their lives that made them heroes to you? Take a moment to reflect on these questions. The ultimate purpose of a life review is to help you answer this question: What *fundamental* concepts do you value most and use to guide your life's direction?

Once you have identified the concepts that are most important to you, you will be better able to answer fundamental questions about your professional future. Where do you see your professional life heading? What do you see as your eventual career and how do you plan to get there? How do you define professional "success"?

Exercise Time

 At this point, complete Exercise 1.1. By writing a one-page narrative describing your personal philosophy of life, you should be able to understand yourself better…and you should develop a better understanding of where you want to go with your professional life.

Exercise 1.1: Personal Philosophy Statement

Use this page (and additional paper, if needed) to describe your personal philosophy of life. Feel free to brainstorm—just let your thoughts go. After all, there are no right or wrong answers when expressing your own philosophy of life.

Once you have finished your personal philosophy statement, review it. Look for keywords that *best* express your personal view of life. After you have identified these keywords, circle or highlight them. Do these keywords indicate anything pertaining to your professional career? If so, write down how these words relate to your career.

_____

_____

_____

_____

_____

_____

_____

_____

_____

_____

_____

_____

_____

_____

_____

_____

_____

_____

Interests and Needs

Soon you will be required to make a very important and perhaps difficult decision—where to do your internship. To make this decision, you should have a good understanding of your own personal and professional interests and needs. What aspects of your personal and professional life add to your happiness? What leisure interests do you have? How important are they to you? What is it about a particular career or job that makes you interested in pursuing it? How important is it for you to work with creative people, to work for an understanding boss, to make a lot of money, to be able to upgrade your skills, to achieve promotions, to live in a small city, to live in a safe community, and so forth? These questions, and others like them, are important to ask yourself *before* you embark on your professional career. They will help you understand what things you need and want from both your personal and professional lives. Meeting your needs and interests may be essential in order for you to continue to be productive in your career and achieve the "success" you are seeking. In Chapter Three, you will have a chance to analyze how well prospective internship sites may meet your personal and professional needs.

Personality Traits and Professional Skills

As an applicant for an internship position, you need to know your personality as well as your professional skills and potential. Over the years, you have developed a wide variety of skills, and each internship supervisor has requirements that must be matched to the skills of prospective interns. If you are to do an effective job of selling yourself to a potential internship supervisor, you must have a thorough understanding of your own personal and professional strengths. By knowing your strengths, you will be able to emphasize them during the application and interview process. Take this opportunity to examine your skills and potential, which will make you a "winner."

The next few pages provide exercises to help you to assess your professional skills and potential as well as your personality traits. When completing these exercises, it is essential to be honest! You might also ask others close to you to review these forms and provide input. Sometimes others seem to know us better than we know ourselves. It is also important that you take your time completing these exercises. If they are done in haste, you will not receive the maximum benefit from them. These exercises intend to help you know yourself, and knowing yourself well is the cornerstone to building a successful professional career.

Exercise Time

 Exercise 1.2 is a Personal and Professional Assessment. Use this form to list your past and present work experiences and some skills you have acquired from each position. Also, list academic skills that you have gained in school and personality traits that you possess. This exercise is open-ended—that is, it allows you to choose descriptions of yourself and your abilities. Once you have completed this exercise, turn to the next pages (Exercises 1.3 and 1.4) and complete the Professional Skills and Personality Traits Assessments. These checklists should help you to expand your awareness of traits and skills that are important for a student intern to possess.

Exercise 1.2: Personal and Professional Assessment

This exercise is designed to assist you in examining your skills, achievements, and personality traits. Reflect on what professional and academic skills you have developed and what personality characteristics you demonstrate. Be honest and thorough in this self-evaluation. Use additional paper if needed.

PROFESSIONAL ASSESSMENT

Experience (Paid or Volunteer)   Skills and Achievements

_____

_____

_____

_____

_____

_____

_____

EDUCATIONAL ASSESSMENT

What relevant skills and knowledge have I gained from my academic studies?

_____

_____

_____

_____

_____

_____

_____

Exercise 1.3: Professional Skills Assessment

Listed below are a variety of professional skills that may be important for you to demonstrate during your internship and throughout your professional career. This form can be used to: (1) identify specific professional skills you possess, plus those you need to refine or acquire; or (2) assess whether your skills match the requirements of the specific internship position you are seeking. This list does not include all possible professional skills. Feel free to add any additional professional skills that you want to assess, especially those important to your professional specialization or option.

Internship Position Title (Optional):				
Professional Skills	Already Possess	Already Possess But Need To Refine	Need To Acquire	Not Needed For Internship
Advising				
Analyzing				
Assessing				
Budgeting				
Communicating (written)				
Communicating (oral)				
Computing				
Conceptualizing				
Consulting				
Coordinating				
Decision Making				
Delegating				
Designing				
Directing				
Documenting				
Evaluating				
Goal Setting				
Initiating				
Instructing				
Leading				
Managing				
Marketing				
Negotiating				
Observing				
Organizing				
Planning				
Problem Solving				
Reporting				
Scheduling				
Selling				
Supervising				
Teaching				
Teamwork				
Writing				

Exercise 1.4: Personality Traits Assessment

Listed below are a variety of personality traits that may be important for you to demonstrate during your internship and throughout your professional career. This form can be used to: (1) identify specific personality traits you possess, plus those you need to refine or acquire; or (2) assess whether your traits match the requirements of the specific internship position you are seeking. This list does not include all possible personality traits. Feel free to add any additional traits/skills that you want to assess, especially those important to your professional specialization or option.

Internship Position Title (Optional):				
Personality Traits	Already Am	Already Am, But Need To Refine	Need To Become	Not Needed For Internship
Able to laugh freely				
Able to say no				
Accepting of criticism				
Communicative				
Confident				
Considerate of others				
Cooperative				
Creative				
Determined				
Dynamic				
Empathic				
Enthusiastic				
Flexible				
Friendly				
Good listener				
Hard worker				
Honest				
Intelligent				
Loyal				
Motivated				
Open-minded				
Patient				
Poised				
Punctual				
Proud				
Reflective				
Reliable				
Resourceful				
Responsible				
Risk taker				
Self-reliant				
Spontaneous				
Stable (emotionally)				
Tactful				

Exercise 1.5: Your Top 10 Assets

Now that you have assessed the professional and personal skills that will help to make you successful, it is important to recognize that some of these skills are more important than others. You need to identify *your* most important assets (i.e., strengths), those that will ensure that you will be a "winner." Review the information you provided in Exercises 1.3 and 1.4. Then, in the space provided below, identify your top ten professional or personal assets. Students rarely have enough examples or descriptions of their assets. Do so in the second column.

Example	Assets
(e.g., Teamwork)	(e.g., Project coordinator for community-wide special event. Coordinated team assignments, meetings, budget and volunteers. Performed final project evaluation.)

Limitations/Weaknesses

Everyone has limitations, and it is important for you to be aware of your personal and professional weaknesses. By knowing your limitations, you will be able to work toward overcoming them. The preceding sections and exercises focused upon identifying your strengths, but they also enabled you to assess areas of weakness. Return to Exercises 1.3 and 1.4 and identify the skills or traits that you need to refine or acquire. Are any of these skills or traits important to success in the type of internship you are seeking? If so, you need to develop a specific plan for overcoming these limitations. During the weeks ahead, set goals that will help you eliminate or diminish these limitations. For example, if you are often late to classes or work, set a *reasonable* goal for next week (e.g., only being late once during the week). If you do not achieve your goal during the first week, keep the goal the same and increase your determination to achieve it. If you *do* achieve your goal for the first week, raise your expectations for the next week, and so on. Establishing reasonable goals and working hard to achieve them can turn limitations into assets.

Professional Use of Technology

The Internet, cell phone, voice/video chat and other technological innovations have dramatically changed the way people communicate with each other, both personally and professionally. Social networks on the Internet (e.g., Twitter, Facebook, Linkedin), for example, are popular ways for students to express themselves, as well as connect with other students and professionals. You should be aware, however, that many personnel departments and potential internship supervisors will check the Internet for information about an applicant. If you have placed unflattering or potentially embarrassing photos or blog content on the Internet, you may lose the internship opportunity you are seeking. Before applying for an internship, be sure to review and "clean up" any unprofessional information contained on social networking sites. Anything that might call into question your moral or ethical character could drop you from an agency's interview list. You should also conduct a vanity search on your name using Google to see what information appears regarding you on the Internet. You might be surprised at what you find.

We also suggest that you open an e-mail account that is used exclusively for internship-related correspondence. Be sure your e-mail address is professional. It sends the wrong message to a potential internship supervisor if your e-mail address prefix is big_stud@ or druglord@. You should also use professional language, not texting language, when corresponding with a potential internship site supervisor via e-mail.

Attitudes Toward Work and Learning

Most internship supervisors mention a student's attitude toward work and learning as being a major factor in their evaluation of the student's performance. Having a positive attitude toward work includes being committed to the position and the agency, understanding and following the agency's philosophy, and being dedicated to the delivery of services and products that benefit the agency. Internship supervisors are looking for students who will carry out and follow through on assigned duties, work well independently *and* with others, and be on time and eager to learn from their work experiences.

The attitudes you display toward work and learning during your internship will help to determine:

- How coworkers feel about you
- How well you rate on internship evaluations
- What type of employment reference letter you will receive after graduation
- How much consideration you will receive for any future job opening with your internship agency

Exercise Time

 It is vital to establish and to continue to demonstrate a positive attitude toward work and toward learning while you are at work. Exercise 1.6 offers you a chance to develop your Work and Learning Attitude Profile. Take the time to write down what you intend to do on your internship that will demonstrate your positive attitude.

Exercise 1.6: Work and Learning Attitude Profile

Reflect on what you are willing to commit to your internship agency. What specific things do you intend to do during your internship that will demonstrate your commitment to the agency, your interest in learning, and your dedication to the quality of your work? Make a list of the actions and behaviors that will demonstrate your *positive attitude* toward work and learning.

_____

_____

_____

_____

_____

_____

_____

_____

_____

_____

_____

_____

_____

_____

_____

_____

_____

_____

_____

Summary

Chapter One formed the foundation for an effective internship search and a successful internship experience. It provided you with information and exercises to examine your personal and professional qualities. Once you have mastered the information in this chapter, you can move ahead with confidence because you have created a sound cornerstone for your internship experience. Knowledge of yourself provides baseline information for establishing internship and career goals, developing a high-quality cover letter and résumé, and preparing for a successful internship interview. Now it is time to move ahead by exploring what *you* want to get from your internship and your professional career.

Chapter Two
Direction

The future belongs to those who believe in the beauty of their dreams.—Eleanor Roosevelt

In the struggle to reach your goals, there is only one way to move: forward.—Maxwell Maltz

This chapter will help you to set internship and career goals to get your career on the right track and help to keep it there. Setting goals is crucial because these goals provide the direction you need to make sound career-related decisions. You might think of this chapter as a road map to your professional future—it enables you to plan your route to success and along the way it serves to keep you on your desired course.

In this chapter, you will identify your internship and career direction by establishing:

- Internship goals
- Career goals
- Action plan timeline

Internship/Career Direction

Even before preparing your résumé or seeking information on internship agencies, it is time to give serious consideration to what you are looking for in your internship and in your professional career. You should ask yourself a few basic questions that will help to clarify your internship and career direction.

Exercise Time

Exercise 2.1 gives you a chance to answer some of these questions and to evaluate how your answers provide direction to your internship and career.

Exercise 2.1: Internship Career Direction

Part A. Questions

For each question below, write your *answer* in the space provided. Then, go back to each question and write down the *direction* (e.g., type of agency and work experiences) your answer suggests you should take to pursue a successful internship and career.

1. What career and educational experiences do I have to build upon?

Answer: _____

_____

_____

Direction: _____

_____

_____

2. At this point, what important career experiences do I lack?

Answer: _____

_____

_____

Direction: _____

_____

_____

3. What type of work do I enjoy most?

Answer: _____

_____

_____

Direction: _____

_____

_____

4. Ultimately, what kind of career position do I want to have?

Answer: _____

_____

_____

Direction: _____

_____

_____

5. What employment choices are viable for me upon graduation?

Answer: _____

_____

_____

Direction: _____

_____

_____

Part B. Internship and Career Direction

Review what you have written for questions 1–5. Then, based upon your *answers* and the *direction* each answer provides, indicate the *ultimate direction* you think your internship and career should take.

_____

_____

_____

_____

_____

_____

_____

_____

Internship Goals

Once you have clarified the direction of your internship and professional career, it is time to establish some concrete goals for your internship. Almost every success story includes statements about the value of setting clear and concise goals. Goals allow you to identify exactly what you want to learn and help you to establish a path for goal attainment. Internship goals, however, do even more than that. When shared with your university's faculty and your agency supervisor, internship goals enable these important people to tailor your internship responsibilities and learning opportunities to fit your needs and interests.

Students sometimes ask us how they can prepare a list of goals before they select their internship site. In fact, it is essential to prepare goals in advance so that you can select a site that offers the kinds of experiences and learning opportunities you need to support your career goals. After you start the internship, you and your agency supervisor should revise your goals based upon agency requirements. However, be sure that most of your internship goals are achievable at the agency you select.

Internship goals can also serve as an unofficial contract that assures you will be taught the work-related skills you need for success in your profession. Ultimately, your primary internship goal is to learn, through experience, as much as possible during your internship. However, it is important to identify *specific* experiences and learning opportunities that you want to have during your internship. Your internship goals should focus upon both what you want to learn (skills and knowledge) and how you want to learn it (experiences). Take time to think realistically about your goals. What things will you be able to learn in the time available? What duties and responsibilities are available to a student intern? What are the essential entry-level skills in your area of specialization? Then, using the information below, develop a comprehensive list of goals that will guide your internship site selection and give specific direction to your internship experience.

Writing Internship Goals

Goals, as used in this manual, are general outcome statements. They specify what you expect to learn and to experience during your internship. Goals are not as specific as objectives, and they are not necessarily observable and measurable. They must, however, be specific enough to allow you and your supervisor to assess whether or not you are achieving your goals. The information that follows should help you to prepare a comprehensive list of goals for your internship:

1. Include generic skills important to any recreation and leisure service professional. These include leadership skills, interpersonal skills, and administrative skills.

2. Identify entry-level skills that are important in your area of specialization. For example, a commercial recreation student's goals may include marketing, selling, and accounting skills, whereas a therapeutic recreation student's goals might include skills related to assessment, documentation, and leisure education.

3. Build upon skills you already possess and identify skills that you need to obtain. Refer to Exercise 2.1, questions 1 and 2 to help you.

4. Whenever possible, include verbs that clarify what you actually plan to *do,* rather than focusing exclusively on what you want to learn. For example, you may be able to learn by observing your supervisor lead activities. However, you would learn more by actually leading activities yourself.

5. Be comprehensive. Make sure that all essential entry-level skills are covered in your list of goals. You do not want to realize too late that your internship did not include experiences vital to securing a job after graduation.

6. Be realistic. Do not include experiences that would not be attainable or available during an internship. For example, a student intern would not actually prepare a departmental budget. However, he or she should be able to learn how the budgeting process works.

Examples of Internship Goals

Carefully review the lists of internship goals provided. We have included examples from a variety of specializations. Therefore, not all of these goals will be appropriate for your career direction. Use these examples for guidance, but be sure to write your goals with *your* experiences and career direction in mind. Also, use your own style and wording when writing goal statements.

INTERNSHIP GOALS—EXAMPLE #1 *Yu Kyoung*

During my internship, I would like to:

1. Select, implement, and evaluate treatment, leisure education, and recreation participation services for clientele
2. Accurately and effectively assess clients' leisure-related needs
3. Develop therapeutic recreation plans with goals and objectives for individual clientele based on assessment
4. Serve as a part of an interdisciplinary team and become knowledgeable about treatment methods and techniques of other allied health disciplines
5. Document client progress regularly, accurately, and efficiently, then modify the therapeutic recreation plans as needed
6. Accurately document each assigned client's status at discharge
7. Gain a greater understanding of the agency and clientele by attending workshops and in-service sessions with particular emphasis on disabling conditions
8. Understand administrative processes utilized in managing a therapeutic recreation facility, including budgeting, reimbursement procedures, staff management, and scheduling
9. Increase my awareness of laws, regulations, and accreditation standards that affect the agency and its clientele

INTERNSHIP GOALS—EXAMPLE #2 *George L. Brooks*

My internship goals are to:

1. Gain knowledge of the administrative operation within the agency and the responsibilities of the staff
2. Develop an understanding of the various financial procedures and budgeting techniques utilized by the agency
3. Organize, plan, and implement recreation/leisure programs that will effectively meet the needs of the individuals served
4. Utilize effective interpersonal skills to demonstrate quality public relations with staff members and the agency's clientele
5. Accurately and efficiently evaluate recreation and leisure programs within the agency
6. Gain direct experience with promotional efforts utilized by the agency, including methods used to channel these efforts to potential clientele
7. Develop an understanding of maintenance procedures involved in efficiently operating the agency's facilities
8. Directly assist with operating concession and vending amenities within the agency
9. Solve problems common to a commercial recreation operation
10. Learn effective methods and procedures for management of human resources in a commercial recreation operation including hiring practices, termination policies, staff evaluation, and in-service training arrangements

11. Gain an understanding of risk management procedures utilized by the agency

12. Gain an appreciation of the qualities needed to be an effective and efficient manager within a commercial operation

INTERNSHIP GOALS—EXAMPLE #3 *Brianna Wixley*

During my internship, I would like to:

1. Participate in the financial aspects involved in operating a public recreation agency, including budgeting and program fee determination

2. Assist administrators (supervisors, program directors) with the duties and responsibilities of the administrator, supervisor, and program director

3. Better understand the overall impact of legal liabilities on a public recreation agency

4. Gain experience in the preparation of a budget for various recreation programs and for a recreation agency

5. Assist with the implementation of an effective public relations strategy within the agency and in the community

6. Plan and conduct various recreation programs for a variety of age groups

7. Create and assist with the distribution of publicity materials for agency programs

8. Learn how to create an efficient and effective overall schedule of programs for a public recreation agency

9. Construct and implement an evaluation tool to determine if selected programs are meeting stated goals and objectives

INTERNSHIP GOALS—EXAMPLE #4 *Jonathon Demby*

My internship goals are to:

1. Use survey methodology to identify outdoor recreation needs and interests of a wide variety of individuals and groups

2. Evaluate the degree to which outdoor recreation programs meet their established goals and objectives

3. Observe and directly participate in three areas of the agency: resource management, administration, and interpretation

4. Better understand the interrelationship between environment/wildlife and human beings with an emphasis on mutually beneficial management techniques

5. Be involved with agency-related resource management projects, such as wildlife inventories, trail maintenance, and patrol and vegetation surveys

6. Demonstrate effective public relations skills by interacting with the public and agency staff in an effective and courteous manner

7. Understand the administration of outdoor programs with emphasis on budgeting staff relations, public relations, and personnel supervision

8. Gain an understanding of facility layout, daily operations, maintenance, equipment, and supplies

9. Learn about the policies and practices of other recreation and park agencies in the area by visiting at least three facilities

10. Become aware of the implications of the state and federal laws and regulations related to outdoor recreation agencies

11. Observe supervisory techniques of selected outdoor recreation professionals to help me become an effective supervisor

Exercise Time

 Once you have completed reviewing our examples, use the form provided in Exercise 2.2 to develop your own list of internship goal statements. Remember, however, that your *final* list of goals to be shared with your faculty and internship supervisor must be prepared in a professional manner.

Exercise 2.2: Internship Goals

Develop *at least* eight goals that you want to accomplish during your internship experience. Be sure that these goals conform to the information provided in this chapter.

Goal #1: _____

_____

_____

Goal #2: _____

_____

_____

Goal #3: _____

_____

_____

Goal #4: _____

_____

_____

Goal #5: _____

_____

_____

Goal #6: _____

_____

_____

Goal #7: _____

_____

_____

Goal #8: _____

_____

_____

Writing Personal Goals

After observing and working with students for over 30 years, the authors consider personal goals to be extremely important. Students and professionals need a quality of life outside of work! In order not to sell yourself to the company 24/7, 365 days, students need personal goals to maintain a balanced life. These personal goals are for your individual growth and development. *A balanced life is a quality life!*

PERSONAL GOALS—EXAMPLE *Yu Kyoung*

During my internship, I will:

1. Maintain healthy eating habits

2. Continue to exercise three to four times a week

3. Improve my ability to speak in public

4. Continue to stay in contact with friends and family

5. Explore the new geographical area I will be living in

Career Goals

Although internship goals are your primary concern at this point in your professional life, it is also important to formulate some career goals. Earlier in this chapter, you answered some questions that helped to provide information about your career direction. Now, you should take the time to develop some career goals that will provide direction for internship selection. As was true of internship goals, career goals should be general outcome statements; however, they have a longer range than internship goals and should indicate a progression as you move along your career path.

Exercise Time

 Exercise 2.3 provides a form to help you to develop some career goals. Using this form, state an overall career goal (what you hope to accomplish during your career) and develop 1- to 2-year and 3- to 5-year goals to help you accomplish your overall career goal. After you have completed Exercise 2.3, check to make sure your career goals are consistent with your career direction information in Exercise 2.1. If not, you may want to revise your goals or reconsider your career direction.

Exercise 2.3: Career Goals

Develop a workable set of goals for your professional career. Be as specific as possible.

Overall Career Goal Statement

_____

_____

_____

_____

Area of Development	1- to 2-Year Goal	3- to 5-Year Goal
Work Environment		
Specific Job Title		
Duties/Responsibilities		
Salary Range		
Benefits		

Action Plan Timeline

So far in this chapter, you have identified your internship goals and career goals. It is now time to develop your action plan for getting the best possible internship—one that will enable you to meet your internship goals *and* get you started toward accomplishing your career goals. In effect, this manual is your internship action plan. It begins with a self-assessment (Chapter One) and systematically takes you through the steps necessary for you to get the internship you want.

At this point, it is important to begin looking ahead to the things you have left to accomplish *before* starting your internship. The best way to do this is by use of an action plan timeline. Constructing and using your timeline involves four steps:

1. Identify all internship-related tasks you need to do between now and when you start your internship.

2. Arrange these tasks in the order you need to start them, beginning with setting your internship goals and progressing through to the start of your internship.

3. Use backward planning techniques to establish deadline dates. These include target dates for finishing each task, and starting dates by which you need to begin working on the task to complete it on time. Beginning at the end of your list, place a target date on your last item. Then, estimate how long it will take to complete the task. Some tasks can be completed on the same day, while others may take weeks to complete. Repeat this process for each task working your way from the bottom of the list to the top. Be sure to set realistic dates for each task.

4. Record your completion date for each task. This is the actual date you completed the task. By monitoring your starting dates and comparing your completion date with the target date, you can easily keep track of your progress.

In developing your timeline, there are some important things to consider. First, allow plenty of time to accomplish each task. Also, while it is important to stay on schedule, you also must remain flexible with many of your target dates. Murphy's Law reminds us that "if anything can go wrong, it will." Thus, you need to be prepared for some setbacks and do not panic if you miss a target date or two. Keep in mind, however, that some dates are not flexible. Examples of inflexible target dates may include your deadline for notifying university personnel of your internship selection and the starting date of your internship.

Exercise Time

 The following example provides a sample timeline with starting and target dates. Review this example and then construct one of your own in Exercise 2.4.

SAMPLE INTERNSHIP TIMELINE			
Task	**Starting Date**	**Target Date**	**Completion Date**
Develop internship and career goals	1/22	1/25	
Research and compile list of potential internship agencies	1/25	2/12	
Discuss potential internships with faculty	2/15	2/19	
Assess personal needs and priorities	2/15	2/19	
Prepare a cover letter	2/19	3/12	
Prepare a résumé	2/19	3/12	
Obtain letters of recommendation	2/21	3/12	
Prepare business cards (if desired)	2/21	3/12	
Develop a portfolio	3/1	3/15	
Attend trainings offered by your universities career center	3/1	3/15	
Participate in mock interviews (if your campus offers them)	3/1	3/15	
Decide on agencies to pursue	3/5	3/6	
E-mail, mail, or phone potential agencies	3/6	3/10	
Make follow-up calls to establish interview dates	3/10	3/25	
Confirm interview dates/times	3/25	3/27	
Select interviewing wardrobe	3/25	3/27	
Participate in interview	3/27	4/15	
Send "thank-you" notes to interviewers	3/27	4/15	
Meet with advisor to help select internship agency	4/15	4/20	
Discuss internship selection with family	4/15	4/20	
Confirm internship and discuss arrangement such as pay, stipend, housing, and starting date	4/15	4/20	
Notify other agencies of internship selection	4/20	4/25	
Register for internship course	4/20	4/25	
Move to internship location	5/5	5/10	
Begin internship	5/10	5/10	

Name: _____

Exercise 2.4: Internship Timeline

Task	Starting Date	Target Date	Completion Date

Summary

Preparing for making decisions and taking action is an important aspect of your internship selection process. A well-conceived action plan, based on sound internship and career goals, is the catalyst for a successful internship experience.

This chapter helped you to develop a clear picture of what you want to achieve from your internship. Now it is time to explore how best to achieve these goals. The search process described in Chapter Three will give you concrete examples of how to begin identifying agencies that will enable you to meet your internship goals.

Chapter Three
Search and Research

Success usually comes to those who are too busy to be looking for it.—Henry David Thoreau

The contact you are looking for might be as close as the next person you meet.—Edward Seagle

This chapter will help you to search for and identify potential internship agencies. Searching for an internship agency can be a frustrating and time-consuming process. A thorough search is well worth the effort, however. If you are systematic and thorough in your search for an internship site, you will end up with the best possible internship—one that helps you accomplish your career goals. This chapter intends to help you search for and identify potential internship sites. Once you have identified some potential agencies, the chapter will give you guidelines for researching each of these agencies in depth.

To conduct a systematic search for internship agencies, you will:

- Identify essential characteristics of potential agencies
- Determine your own needs and preferences for an internship site
- Prioritize your needs and preferences
- Identify resources for information on agencies meeting essential characteristics
- Compile a short list of potential agencies that meet essential characteristics and correspond with your needs and preferences
- Seek information on the internship application process by conducting an informational interview

---

Search

The first step in searching for an internship site is to decide what types of agencies or organizations would meet your needs. The preceding chapters have helped you to examine yourself and your career direction. Now you must identify potential internship sites that offer the experiences you need or want. It is important to keep in mind that your search process does not need to include time-consuming, in-depth examination of each potential agency—that will come later. For now, just concentrate upon getting enough information to reduce your alternatives to a manageable number (e.g., five to eight agencies).

Search Step #1: Identify Essential Characteristics of Agencies

You should begin your search process by (1) determining the type of agency or organization that corresponds with your professional interests, and (2) considering your requirements regarding geographic location of the agency or organization. In the next step, we will provide you with a list of other considerations to help narrow your alternatives, but at first it is important to keep your search as broad as possible.

Type of Agency or Organization

First, of course, you probably want to identify sites that offer leisure services corresponding with your option or emphasis area (e.g., commercial recreation, outdoor recreation). You should also consider whether or not you need an internship offering a specific specialization within your option. For example, you may be studying outdoor recreation and specializing in historical interpretation. For you, an essential characteristic of any agency is that it provides historical interpretive services. Or you may be planning to work in therapeutic recreation specializing in physical rehabilitation. You would, therefore, need to identify organizations that have Certified Therapeutic Recreation Specialists and offer physical rehabilitation services. Make sure, however, that any specialization you identify is essential to your professional goals. If you have a preference for a given specialization, but it is not essential, consider it in Step #2 of the search process.

Geographic Location of Agency or Organization

Many students feel limited by geographic considerations. Due to family constraints, interpersonal relationships, financial considerations, or preferences for certain climates, they want to confine their search for an internship site to a specific city, state, or region of the country. It is important to remember, however, that this step in the search process focuses on essential characteristics of agencies. If you are preparing for a career in ski resort management, for example, limiting your search to cold weather climates is essential. Moreover, a few universities require that an internship be confined to a specific region or state. However, some factors that seem essential may not be. For example, financial need may be overcome with an internship that pays a salary. Before limiting your internship search to a specific geographic area, try to make sure that this limitation really is essential. If it is not essential, consider it in Step #2 of the search process. You will use these essential characteristics of a potential internship agency to complete the Internship Selection Priority Form (Exercise 3.3, p. 51).

Search Step #2: Determine Your Own Needs and Preferences

This stage of the search process focuses upon identifying and prioritizing (1) personal internship needs and preferences and (2) profession-related internship needs and preferences. Your personal and professional needs are interdependent and will help you to determine the best personal and professional "fit" for your internship. You should identify as many needs and preferences as possible.

Personal Needs and Preferences

The first two chapters of this manual helped you to identify your own personal and professional strengths and weaknesses as well as career direction and interests. Now this information will be helpful in determining your own internship needs and preferences. Return to these two chapters and review each of the exercises that you completed. In addition to reviewing these exercises, the following additional questions need to be answered regarding your personal needs and preferences.

Exercise Time

The Personal Needs and Preferences Form (Exercise 3.1) gives you some specific questions to answer. Your answers will identify specific personal needs and preferences that may influence your selection of an internship site.

Exercise 3.1: Personal Needs and Preferences Form

The following list of questions will help you to identify factors to consider when selecting potential internship agencies. Circle "yes" or "no" depending upon your own personal needs or preferences.

1. Do I need financial or other assistance during my internship?   Yes   No

    a. Do I need free housing provided by the agency?   Yes   No

    b. Do I need to have free meals provided by the agency?   Yes   No

    c. Do I need to receive payment (stipend/salary) for my internship?   Yes   No

2. Will I need transportation to/from the agency?   Yes   No

3. Do I have significant others that I want to be near during my internship?   Yes   No
   If so, specify who they are and where they live.

4. Do I prefer a specific geographic location for my internship?   Yes   No
   If yes, what specific region, state, or city?

5. Do I want specific leisure opportunities to be available for me   Yes   No
   at or near my internship site?
   If yes, what specific leisure opportunities?

6. Do I prefer to spend most of my workday out-of-doors?   Yes   No

List any additional personal needs or preferences.

_____

_____

_____

_____

_____

_____

_____

Profession-Related Needs and Preferences

Not only must your personal-related needs and preferences be taken into account when evaluating an internship site, but also your professional needs must be evaluated to assess whether a given internship site will meet your needs.

Exercise Time

By completing the Profession-Related Needs and Preferences Form (Exercise 3.2), you will help to clarify some specific needs and preferences that your internship should provide.

Exercise 3.2: Profession-Related Needs and Preferences Form

The following list of questions will help you to identify factors to consider when selecting potential internship agencies. Circle "yes" or "no" depending upon your own profession-related needs or preferences.

1. Do I need a nearby university for supervision or coursework?   Yes   No

2. Is the size of the agency important to my career goals?   Yes   No
   If yes, what size agency am I seeking?

3. Do I want experiences in a specific specialization?   Yes   No
   If yes, what specialization?

4. Am I interested in a specialization with certification requirements?   Yes   No
   If yes, what specific requirements must be met?

5. Do I want to work with a specific population (e.g., adults, at-risk youth)?   Yes   No
   If yes, what specific population(s)?

6. Do I want a site with good post-internship job possibilities?   Yes   No

7. Should my internship provide opportunities different from   Yes   No
   my past experience?

8. Do I need to have a lot of close supervision during my workday?   Yes   No

List any additional profession-related needs or preferences.

_____

_____

_____

_____

_____

_____

_____

_____

_____

Search Step #3: Prioritize Your Needs and Preferences

Now that you have identified your needs and preferences for your internship, it is important to decide which of these items are the most important to you. To do this, review the two forms (Exercises 3.1 and 3.2) you have just completed as part of Step #2. Identify all items receiving a "yes" response, plus those that you have added at the end of each form.

Exercise Time

After identifying all "yes" responses plus your additions on Exercises 3.1 and 3.2, use the Internship Selection Priority Form (Exercise 3.3) to list the 8 to 10 needs and preferences that are most important to your selection of an internship site. Start with the most important item (either profession-related or personal), then list the second most important, and so on. Keep in mind that your internship selection is one of the most important decisions you will make during your academic career. It often determines what direction your professional career takes. Therefore, you should want to place particular emphasis on your profession-related needs and preferences.

Exercise 3.3: Internship Selection Priority Form

First, list the essential criteria identified in Search Step #1. Then, use the Profession-Related Needs and Preferences Form and Personal Needs and Preferences Form to select your most important criterion for an internship site. The most important criterion can be either profession-related or personal, but keep in mind that your internship is important to your professional career. Then list the second most important criterion (either profession-related or personal), and so on.

Essential Criteria

Type of agency or organization (include specialization): _____

_____

_____

_____

Geographic location (if essential): _____

_____

_____

_____

Needs and Preferences

Priority #1: _____

_____

_____

Priority #2: _____

_____

_____

Priority #3: _____

_____

_____

Priority #4: _____

_____

_____

Priority #5: _____

_____

_____

Priority #6: _____

_____

_____

Priority #7: _____

_____

_____

Priority #8: _____

_____

_____

Priority #9: _____

_____

_____

Priority #10: _____

_____

_____

Search Step #4: Identify Resources for Information on Agencies

This section will assist you in identifying many different sources from which to gather internship information. When looking for an internship, you should use all sources. Also, remember anyone you speak with could be a lead to the internship position you want. Stay alert, and be ready to market yourself to anyone at any time. You can never be certain where potential leads might come from, or where they might lead.

What are the resources available to you in your area? This is the time to take stock of the resources that will assist you in finding the internship you want. Following are some of the more commonly used and widely available resources that may be of use.

Faculty

Your department's faculty members know a lot about people and agencies providing leisure services. Let your internship coordinator, faculty advisor, and other faculty members know about your professional interests. Ask them to assist with your search for an internship site that meets your needs. It is important, however, not to depend solely on their help. Using all of the resources available to you will help you to get the best internship for you. Moreover, a thorough search will help when you begin your job search after graduation.

Professionals

Professionals in recreation and leisure are an excellent resource, especially if they are alumni of your college or university. However, do not wait until you are hunting for an internship to get acquainted. Establish a network early. Come up with a strategy for getting to know specific professionals. For example, you might ask to conduct an "informational" interview regarding a specific topic, or regarding opportunities in the field. (Do not ask them for an internship or job at this time.) This allows the professional to get to know you before you ask for help with your internship. Professionals usually do not mind giving their assistance if you make specific requests and act in a professional manner.

Placement and Internship Centers

Most colleges and universities have job placement centers available to students. Some also have centers that focus exclusively on internships. Become acquainted with these offices and their staff members early in your college career. Placement and internship offices can offer information in many ways. For example, they provide career placement counseling and testing to those who find it difficult to get started, who feel they are not in tune with themselves and what they have to offer, or who are highly apprehensive about the internship or job search process. They can provide assistance in locating resource directories, identifying alumni employed in leisure services, and writing cover letters and résumés. They may also set up practice interviews, give information on professional grooming skills, and offer other strategies regarding internships and employment.

The Internet

It is important for you to access the Internet if you want to do a thorough search for internship opportunities. Although the number and scope of internship and job-related databases are changing rapidly, we have included some important websites in Appendix A. These websites, plus use of Internet search engines (e.g., Google, Bing), should allow you to find internship-related resources and databases. Twitter, Facebook, e-mail and live chat, as well as other online collaborative environments, have revolutionized how students and professionals interact. Remember, when searching the Internet for possible internships, use as many variations of the typical job title as possible (e.g., event planner, special events, program, entertainment, wedding planner, coordinator, manager). Also, remember that online classified ad sites such as Craigslist and Backpage may offer useful resources for finding internships.

Using Social Media

Although there are a number of databases with recreation-related internship listings (see Appendix A, p. 179), the traditional approach of mailing a cover letter and résumé to an agency is becoming obsolete. Times have changed and your approach to getting "you" out in front of a potential organization requires different approaches. Some examples of contemporary approaches to try include:

Create an eportfolio. An eportfolio is a website that "showcases" who you are and your capabilities. As part of your application process, it is always good to share your eportfolio, as well as include the URL on your business card. An effective eportfolio will include a professional picture of you and a short bio. It will also include your résumé, a showcase of your capabilities (e.g., photos, videos, files and descriptions of your work to include writing samples, projects and initiatives) and, perhaps, a blog. The eportfolio should also include references (and reference letters), job evaluations, and personal contact information for how to reach you. The eportfolio is not designed to be an online website of your résumé, but rather an expansion of your résumé that demonstrates successful work and action on your part.

Some good examples of eportfolios include:

> http://www.webcitation.org/658XM2NEB
> http://kmrit.weebly.com/
> http://dlw5102.weebly.com/
> http://nicolewells.weebly.com/

Conduct a People Search instead of a Job Search. Most internships/jobs are not posted online. Many companies know who they may want to hire before even posting a position. As studies have shown, approximately 80% of employment is a result of networking. Thus, searching for people that you may want to intern with may lead you to the agency that you will apply to for an internship. Follow these three simple steps:

1. *Select Potential Internship Agencies.* Use indeed.com, Google, Bing or other search engines to help to identify the top five to eight agencies with which you might like to intern.

2. *Conduct a social media or people search.* Use social media or people searches to find people who work at your "top" companies. By using Branchout, Facebook (whodoyouknow on Facebook), Twitter, Linkedin and other social media outlets, you can find and contact employees without needing to "friend," "follow," and the like. Also, websites like Wink, Peekyou, and PPL offer ways to find agency employees. In today's world, it is okay to contact someone through social media outlets without invitation provided that your contact is professional and not overbearing.

3. *Contact the person(s) directly.* Without asking for an internship, let the person know who you are, your interest in finding an internship, and begin to make a "connection." After a few exchanges, ask the person if his or her organization has any internship opportunities and, if not, someone that they can refer you to in order to further your internship pursuit. Make sure that you are specific in your request. Such requests as "I want to learn everything you know about marketing" and "can you share your experience" are too broad, often resulting in little or no response.

Brand Yourself. Utilize Twitter, Facebook, Linkedin, and blog sites to create your professional brand. Complete your profiles 100%, and begin "linking" with others who have interests and/or businesses in your area of interest. Consider upgrading to maximize your exposure and find others who are committed to social media networking.

Construct a Video Résumé and Upload it to YouTube. If you want to enable potential supervisors to get a more personal understanding of your capabilities, you may want to consider creating a video résumé. While many video résumés are good, many others are so rehearsed, poorly choreographed and amateurish that the video résumé actually undermines its purpose and detracts from a candidate's application. If you want to create a video résumé, look at some of the examples on YouTube. Your video should also be short, explain why you are a good candidate for an internship, and present your background in storybook manner. Make sure that your video résumé is of high quality before uploading. Retake as many times as is needed to put your "best self" forward.

Subscribe to Really Simple Syndication (RSS) Feeds. RSS feeds from websites aligned with your professional area of interest can keep you up to date on trends, business developments, political relationships, emerging topical areas and more. By reading RSS feeds, you will be able to talk with knowledge about professionally related current events during interviews, and intelligently share your perspectives within social media networks.

Subscribe to blogs that have job listings. Think about subscribing to or creating a blog in your area of interest that offers internship or job postings. Problogger, for example, offers blogging jobs, and Mashable has a job board highlighting jobs in social media and technology. Sites like Jobamatic offer job postings. Use Google to search for blogs in your area of interest, then narrow your blog search to blogs that have job and/or internship job boards. Contribute to the blogs to gain professional recognition.

Offer your expertise. Social networking is a two-way street. Make sure that you answer questions asked by other students and professionals and/or offer your opinion, advice, or perspective when appropriate. Don't just ask for favors or participate when you want something. Your visibility is important as a contributor.

Social Networking "DO NOTS"

- Do not have your parent or a friend call, e-mail or represent themselves as you. These tactics are quite transparent and convey a message about your inability to independently conduct business.

- Do not pretend to have the same interests as someone that you find in a social media platform. Eventually, you will be "exposed," especially if you are pretending that you have a deep interest in areas not usually associated, such as entomology AND baking brownies.

- Do not criticize other professionals or use unprofessional or inappropriate language. Always be respectful, even if the other person is not.

- Do not post photos of yourself that could be interpreted as distasteful in any way. A picture of you scantily dressed, funneling beer during a tailgate or homecoming party will only serve to create a negative impression. Guaranteed.

- Do not "stalk" a professional. In one case, a student found out where a person was located after he tweeted his current location and the student "accidently" bumped into him at that location asking for an interview. In another case, a "potential candidate" showed up with flowers and requested a date following the interview. Such overly assertive gestures are sure to result in a quick elimination from the candidate pool.

Resource Directories

Directories are a good way to find out about potential internship agencies. A wide variety of specialized organizations publish directories for distribution to their membership. Generally, these directories give the names and business addresses of members or member organizations and sometimes provide details about the agencies listed.

Libraries

Libraries have many resources, including reference books, government publications, directories, telephone books, newspapers, magazines, and other pertinent information on internships and employment. If needed, assistance can be obtained from the reference librarian. Although he or she may not be immediately aware of opportunities in recreation and leisure services, reference librarians are experts in helping people find the resources they need.

Newspapers

Few internships are advertised in city newspapers; however, closely monitoring classified ads may increase your awareness of leisure services agencies and help you with your job search following graduation. Keep in mind, however, that only 10% of potential jobs are listed in the newspaper. Beyond classified ads, city newspapers are excellent resources for learning about new leisure-related businesses in town, identifying key leisure professionals and established businesses, and determining emerging trends and growth patterns. All of these may assist your search for an internship and help to identify employment possibilities. Also, most colleges and universities have student-run newspapers, and some of these do have classified ads and articles about internships in leisure services.

Magazines and Journals

Magazines and journals in recreation and leisure services are often overlooked as resources. Examples of magazines and journals include *Parks & Recreation*, *Journal of Leisure Research*, *Journal of Leisurability* (Canada), *Journal of Parks and Recreation Administration*, *Therapeutic Recreation Journal*, *Leisure Sciences*, *Palaestra*, and *Journal of Physical Education, Recreation and Dance*. Many state recreation and park societies/associations also publish their own magazines, as do some trade organizations. Although magazines and journals do not generally carry ads for internships, they can help you become aware of opportunities, identify key professionals, and target innovative programs within your specialty. When reviewing any magazine or journal, look at all aspects of the document including articles, advertisements, and promotions.

Social Groups (Clubs/Fraternities/Sororities)

Social groups are an instant network of people who share your interests. You may also want to investigate groups in your area that can be of benefit to you, socially and professionally. Share yourself with others and begin to make contacts. Develop your network. An excellent place to start is your school's student-run recreation and park society.

Professional Organizations

Becoming part of a professional organization assists with your professional development. Such organizations include your state's recreation and park society/association, National Recreation and Park Association, Club Managers Association of America, National Therapeutic Recreation Society, American Therapeutic Recreation Association, and the National Intramural–Recreational Sports Association. Leisure-related state and national organizations, with contact information, are provided in Appendix B (p. 185). Involvement in a professional organization indicates your commitment to leisure services, and allows full-time professionals to view your enthusiasm and expertise. Involvement now may not only help you find an internship, but also assist you in finding employment in the field after graduation.

Newsletters

A variety of electronic newsletters are published by organizations in leisure services. Most professional organizations have their own newsletter, and these often have information on members and organization activities. Job listings and internship information are sometimes included in newsletters. Since these newsletters are generally only distributed to members, you should check with your faculty to see what memberships they hold. A wide variety of leisure service agencies also publish their own newsletters, which generally focus upon the activities of their staffs and consumers. Although an agency-specific newsletter may not help you identify a variety of potential internship sites, it will assist you in learning more about a particular agency.

Conferences

Conferences are a good place to network with fellow students and full-time professionals. If obtaining an internship (or employment) is a reason you are attending a conference, be prepared to market yourself. If not, go with the idea of expanding your established network of people. If you have already prepared your résumé, be sure to take plenty of copies with you. Whenever you talk with persons who have internship leads, or may serve as resource persons, ask for a business card. When you receive a business card, do not just put it away, but turn it over and write some notes about your conversation with the person. This will make it easier to recall the conversation and the individual at a later date. Many conferences also have internship and job marts that provide valuable information on internships and employment in leisure services. For information on upcoming conferences, check with your faculty or contact the professional organizations listed in Appendix B (p. 185).

Friends/Relatives

Take time to convey your aspirations to people close to you. Many times your friends and relatives may not be aware of your chosen career or what you hope to achieve in your professional life. However, these people have your best interest at heart. If you are seeking an internship from a specific geographic location, consider where your relatives live. Be sure that your relative is a willing partner in your internship pursuit and ensure that you do not wear out your "welcome."

Internship or Job Announcements

Internship and job announcements (e.g., e-mail announcements, bulletins, descriptions) are often sent to faculty by potential supervisors. Also, many professional organizations send internship and electronic job bulletins to members or subscribers. Check with your faculty to see what bulletins they receive. When reviewing internship and job announcements you should go beyond looking only at the job title, pay, and benefits. Go over the entire announcement carefully. Identify key points. Doing this can give you a clearer idea as to what the potential internship supervisor or employer is looking for in an applicant, and will give you an edge over other applicants because you are prepared. Also, identify some questions from the announcement you can ask during an interview. Use a colored marker to highlight areas you want to review later. Those areas marked may be formed into interview questions that you could practice before the actual interview.

Employment Agencies

Employment agencies are usually expensive and do not have information on internships. You can do just as good a job of finding an internship (or job) if you follow the recommendations given in this manual. However, employment agencies sometimes do have employment listings that do not show up in other resources.

Networking

Networking involves establishing communication links between you and other individuals, groups, and agencies. It is the art of building alliances. Networking starts long before a job search, and you probably don't even realize you are doing it. Everyone is a potential resource, so use all the resources at your disposal. Your networking strategy should have the same effect as dropping a stone in water. When the stone hits the water, a rippling effect takes place, with the ripples expanding wider and wider. That is what your network should be. Every person you interact with is a contact and a potential lead. Learning how to develop and nurture a professional network will benefit you throughout your professional career (see *Networking: The Art of Building Alliances*).

Networking: The Art of Building Alliances

- In social or professional gatherings, make your initial contact with someone who is not currently interacting with others
- Introduce yourself and smile as you shake hands
- Don't be afraid to ask, "What do you do?"
- Ask for a business card to help you keep track of contacts
- Listen attentively and keep alert for potential leads
- Don't get discouraged if your initial efforts do not seem to be successful
- Persevere—the connection you fail to make may have been the perfect lead to your ideal internship
- Use a systematic method to record your contact (see *Contact Record Sheet* on p. 61)
- Constantly nurture your network by maintaining contact with those you have met

---

Today, networking occurs on two distinct levels—human and electronic. Human networking involves direct interaction among people, and it is still the most popular method of finding an internship or job. It is estimated, for example, that between 70% and 80% of all jobs are acquired through word of mouth. Another way to enhance your human network is through the use of a business card. An example of a business card developed by a student can be seen in *Business Cards for Students,* p. 59.

E-mail also provides a quick and economical way to communicate, and e-mail networks enable everyone on a given network to get information almost instantly. To link with an existing e-mail network in recreation and leisure services, contact your university's faculty for advice or search the Internet for helpful e-mail addresses. Some of the organizations in Appendix B also have their own networks. Social networks on the Internet should be used with caution (see Professional Use of Technology on p. 15).

The Contact Record Sheet provides a system to track your internship contacts. This chart is simple to use and keeps key people within reach for continuous contact. Enter information into your PDA or cell phone. You may want to copy the Contact Record Sheet to record additional contacts.

Search Step #5: Compile a List of Potential Internship Agencies

Now that you have completed the previous tasks, it is time to begin your search for specific agencies or organizations that meet your essential criteria (Step #1) and offer as many of your prioritized needs and preferences as possible (Step #3). Using your resources (Step #4), identify internship sites that meet your essential criteria; then, compare your prioritized needs and preferences with what each site offers. Compile a list of agencies that appear to offer you what you are looking for in an internship agency.

Be selective. Don't try to list every agency or organization. If an agency appears to be a good prospect for you because it meets the most important items on your prioritized list, include it. Your final list of potential internship agencies should include five to eight agencies that are the best fit with your prioritized needs and preferences. Once you have this list, you are well on you way to finding your ideal internship site.

Search Step #6: Conduct an Informational Interview

Before delving into what each agency has to offer, you should examine the internship application process *from the perspective of an internship supervisor*. Granted, perspectives may vary from supervisor to supervisor, but gathering information from someone who has experience with supervision of interns should help you throughout your internship quest.

Business Cards for Students

Here is a sample business card that students might use to increase their networking potential.

Front of Business Card

Kelly Bloom

Recreation and Park Management
Southern State University
Graduation Date: May 2014

34 Shadow Lane
Wilema, NC 23941
Tel: 815.879.1100
Email: kbloom@ssu.edu

Back of Business Card

Certified Wilderness First Responder
Environmental Interpreter
Rock Climbing Instructor
Trip Leader
Camp Counselor
24-mile Marathoner

Bilingual: Spanish
Computer Proficient: Microsoft Office, Camtasia, HTML, Web 2.0

Exercise Time

Identify a local professional who has supervised at least one student from your university. You might select him or her from the list of agencies you compiled above (Search Step #5), or you could seek assistance from fellow students or your university's internship coordinator. Regardless of how you identify this professional, it is best to select someone whom you do *not* intend to contact for an internship. Next, call the professional and request an informational interview to help you learn more about the internship application process. The interview should take no more than one hour and should focus on the questions included in the Informational Interview Form (Exercise 3.4, p. 63).

Contact Record Sheet

contact person
_____

company name
_____

street
_____

city
_____

state   zip   phone number
_____

fax number   e-mail

date cover letter/résumé submitted
_____

notes
_____
_____
_____
_____
_____
_____
_____
_____

---

contact person
_____

company name
_____

street
_____

city
_____

state   zip   phone number
_____

fax number   e-mail

date cover letter/résumé submitted
_____

notes
_____
_____
_____
_____
_____
_____
_____
_____

---

contact person
_____

company name
_____

street
_____

city
_____

state   zip   phone number
_____

fax number   e-mail

date cover letter/résumé submitted
_____

notes
_____
_____
_____
_____
_____
_____
_____
_____

Exercise 3.4: Informational Interview Form

The following is a list of questions you might ask during your informational interview. An informational interview is conducted with a professional in the career field that you desire to intern and should last a minimum of 20 minutes. The purpose of the interview is to help you prepare for your internship, so be sure to ask the questions most relevant to you.

- How should prospective interns make contact with you and your agency?

_____

_____

- How do you choose prospective interns to interview?

_____

_____

- How do you notify prospective interns of their interview time?

_____

_____

- What should prospective interns do to prepare for their interview?

_____

_____

- Should prospective interns bring anything to the interview?

_____

_____

- Is it important for interviewees to obtain information about your agency in advance?

_____

_____

- What do you look for in a cover letter?

_____

_____

- What do you look for in a résumé?

_____

_____

- What kind of interviews do you prefer (e.g., one-on-one, panel)?

_____

_____

- How should a interviewee dress?

_____

_____

- What are some examples of questions you often ask interviewees?

_____

_____

- Do you prefer situational or problem-solving questions?

_____

_____

- Do you ask an interviewee to provide examples of their written work?

_____

_____

- Do applicants need any specialized credentials, such as First Aid or CPR?

_____

_____

- How long do your interviews usually last?

_____

_____

- How much importance do you place upon written letters of reference?

_____

_____

- What kind and how many references do you recommend?

_____

_____

- What things can applicants do during the application process to enhance their chances of getting an internship with your agency?

_____

_____

- Describe the process you use to make your decision on an applicant.

_____

_____

- Does anyone assist you in making hiring decisions on interns?

_____

_____

- Should the applicant send a thank-you letter after an interview? If so, what should it say?

_____

_____

- Any other points that you think I should know that would assist me in the hiring/employment process?

_____

_____

Be creative and ask additional questions that get you the information you want.

Research

Once you have identified your priorities, reduced your list of potential internship agencies to a manageable number, and learned more about the application process, it is time to begin an *intensive, agency-specific* research process. This process intends to give you as much information as possible about your potential agencies *before* making formal application for an internship. How do you get this information? You may need to read agency brochures or reports, job descriptions/announcements, financial statements, visit the organization, and talk with people who work at the agency.

Start the research process with the agency that appears to offer you the best possible internship, but do not confine your research to a single agency. You should gather detailed information on at least three to five of your preferred agencies. Your research is crucial—it enables you to get the information you need to select your internship site. It also allows you to show the "best you" to potential internship supervisors. Internship supervisors are looking for well-prepared students who can sell themselves and their abilities. Gaining information about a potential internship agency before an interview will give you an edge in your quest for the best possible internship.

University Files and Resources

Some universities maintain extensive files on prospective internship agencies. These files often contain detailed information on an agency, such as annual reports, newsletters, promotional materials, or agency descriptions written by previous interns. Check with your internship coordinator or university internship office to see if files exist for the agencies on your list. Many universities also have a career services office that may maintain relevant files. If so, make sure that the materials are thorough and up-to-date. If no files exist or the materials are out-of-date, you may have to make direct contact with the agency to gather the information that you need.

Agency Websites

Many agencies offering internships have their own websites. Detailed information on these agencies and their services may be available here. Also, some internship databases provide thumbnail sketches of listing agencies, with a direct link to homepages for agencies with Internet addresses. Appendix A includes many useful websites.

Telephone Calls

The telephone is useful in gaining information about an agency and determining to whom your cover letter and résumé should be sent. A phone call also may reveal that an agency is not accepting interns, thus allowing you to concentrate your efforts on other agencies. Be assertive, but not aggressive in your preliminary informational telephone calls. If using a cell phone, make sure that you are in a quiet space with good reception. The agency does not want to hear your roommate, music, a barking dog, or any other distracting noises. Also, by asking for exactly what you want (e.g., promotional brochures, newsletters, annual reports, name of recreation director), you are more likely to be helped. You may have to call more than once to get the name of the person or the information you need. Be ready to sell yourself in the event you are transferred directly to a potential internship supervisor. He or she may want to conduct an internship interview right on the spot; however, it is better to explain that you are still researching agencies and would prefer to set up a formal interview at a later date. Unless you are certain that this agency is ideal for you, it is important not to make commitments during your research process.

Voice Mail

You need to be prepared to leave a message via voice mail if the person you wish to speak with is unavailable. You may even want to write down and practice (do not read) your voice mail message prior to phoning a prospective internship agency. In your voice mail message, introduce yourself and give your complete phone number. Give a clear and concise message, perhaps including who referred you or how you learned about the agency. At the end of the message, you may want to repeat your name and phone number again. Be sure to thank the person, then hang up promptly. Throughout your message, speak slowly and distinctly so the person has time to write down the information you provide. If you leave your phone number for someone to call you back, make sure *your* voice mail message is professional in content and tone.

E-Mail

E-mail is an effective tool if used properly. A well-written request letter allows you to make a good first impression and enables you to specify exactly what information you want. Remember, a specific request is harder to ignore than a vague one. Directing e-mail to a specific individual is recommended, but be certain that you know the person's correct title and correct spelling of his or her name. Also, ensure that you write your e-mails in a professional and grammatically correct manner. Absence of spelling and grammatical errors, slang, and texting language should be your goal. Do not just e-mail your request and wait indefinitely. After a preplanned period of time—two to three weeks—make a follow-up telephone call. Check to make sure the agency received your request for information. If the information has not yet been sent, ask when you might expect to receive it.

Internship (Job) Description

Some agencies provide "job descriptions" for their internship positions. These can be extremely valuable as you search for potential internship agencies. Internship supervisors put a lot of work into their internship descriptions and include information you can use to determine if a given internship site is right for you. An internship description might include the following:

- Position description. Provides an overview of the position and what is expected of potential interns.
- Responsibilities.
  - Essential duties. Key duties you must be able to perform in relations to that specific internship.
  - Nonessential duties. Other duties you may be asked to perform, but are not essential to that specific internship.
- Knowledge and critical skills. Amount of knowledge required to accomplish critical aspects of the internship.
- Education. Level of education (i.e., class standing) required to qualify for the internship.
- Experience. Types of experiences that the agency will expect students to have in order to succeed in the internship.
- License or certification eligibility. Completion of specific academic requirements in order to be eligible for licensure or certification following the internship.
- Additional Qualifications. Having specific foreign language skills, computer skills, etc.
- Physical requirements. Essential physical abilities that an applicant will have to possess in order to perform internship-related tasks.
- Work schedule. Weekly hours required to meet expectations of the agency.
- Benefits overview. What benefits, if any, are provided for interns (e.g., health or liability insurance, compensatory time, housing, or food allowance).
- How to apply. Steps or information to assist you in applying for the internship.
- Final filing or closing date. The date all internship related materials need to be received by the agency.
- Agency description. Agency might include some information about the agency, their philosophy, programs, services, and demographic information.
- Equal opportunity statement. That the agency complies with state and national laws related to hiring.

Once you receive a copy of the internship description, take the time to review it thoroughly. You might take a couple markers (e.g., yellow, blue, pink) and highlight specific responsibilities and other important information that you can use in your cover letter and, eventually, your interview. Make one of the color markers primary to highlight the most important skills and information, and another color for secondary skills and information. By doing this you will become more confident in what skills are expected of interns, as well as how you match up to those skills.

Visit Site

If possible, visit the site before your interview to better prepare yourself. By making a visitation you will (1) know how to get there and how long it will take, (2) be aware of the atmosphere of the company-formal or informal, (3) perhaps run into someone you know who could put in a good word for you, (4) meet the receptionist and establish rapport early, and (5) obtain additional information for your use. Also, an informational site visit may reveal that this agency really is not what you are looking for in an internship site.

Making a Pre-interview Appointment

If you are seeking employment at an internship site, you may want to make a pre-interview appointment with the person who will be conducting interviews. This will help clarify any information you may need for the upcoming interview. If a pre-interview appointment is not possible, but you are able to speak with the receptionist, ask for the name of the person who will be conducting the interview and then ask for him or her by name when you arrive for your interview. People like to be called by name, but be sure not to be too informal.

Contacts Within the Agency

If you know anyone familiar with the agency, talk to him or her about the company's philosophy, goals, future plans, and anything else about the agency. The better you know the company, the better you will do in an interview and the better the chance that you will select the internship site that is right for you.

Speak with Current or Past Interns at the Agency

If you know current or past interns at the agency, talk to them for another perspective on the agency. This information will help to ensure that the agency can meet your professional goals. It may also assist you in your interview and increase your knowledge of specific jobs available to interns. Be prepared with questions, and thank them for their assistance.

Volunteer at the Agency

Many recreation and leisure agencies need volunteer help to support their programs and activities. Volunteering for at least one program will enable you to get to know the agency and its services firsthand. Volunteering is time-consuming, but it is worth it. It not only provides you with information, but it allows you to demonstrate your knowledge and skills to important agency personnel. Volunteering also adds to your résumé, even if you decide against applying for an internship at that agency.

Summary

This chapter provided a systematic process for identifying potential internship agencies and narrowing your selections to a manageable number of sites. Learning how to search for an internship site, including identification of resources and networking, is a necessary strategy. Effective networking is especially valuable, now and in the future. You should continue to network throughout your career.

This chapter also identified ways to research information you need to consider in your internship selection process. Becoming familiar with an agency before you make contact, and especially before your internship interview, can give you an edge. Sometimes your research reveals that this isn't the agency for you, but it can also confirm that this is your ideal agency.

Now it is time to combine the chapters that you have completed and to develop the tools that will market your talents and abilities. The next two chapters will assist you in developing essential internship tools, or aid in the refinement of tools you already have. Remember, completing the preceding chapters is vital for developing high-quality internship tools.

Chapter Four
Preparation: The Cover Letter

All action has its roots in communication.—Randy Bens

It is very easy to turn directly to this chapter, skipping the others, in your haste to get started in your internship preparation. If you have done so, you have missed the chapters that can give you the edge over other applicants. This chapter is important because the end result is your first formal communication with the prospective internship supervisor—your cover letter. However, what leads up to this point is vital to your success. If you have not read Chapters One through Three (and completed the exercises they contain), you should return to the beginning of the manual and start from there.

> **To develop your cover letter, you need to:**
> * Understand acceptable formats for a cover letter
> * Know the appropriate content of a cover letter
> * Review examples of cover letters

The cover letter is the letter you write to potential internship sites to inform them of your interest and to let them know that your résumé is enclosed for their review. It is more than a formality—it is crucial. According to the Society of Human Resource Management (SHRM),"76 percent of employers may automatically eliminate an employment candidate from any further hiring consideration based solely on the quality of his/her cover letter" (SHRM.org).

The cover letter offers a chance for you to let a potential internship supervisor know that you are truly excited about his or her agency and the prospect of learning from him or her. The cover letter also gives you the opportunity to demonstrate that you have an essential skill: the ability to communicate clearly and effectively in writing. Moreover, the cover letter allows you to create interest by matching your skills with the requirements of a given internship. When a potential internship supervisor reads your cover letter, you want him or her to know that you are enthusiastic, bright, energetic, and qualified.

Format of a Cover Letter

Since the cover letter is so important, it is your task to create a cover letter that looks professional and catches the potential internship supervisor's eye. Even before beginning to read your cover letter, a potential internship supervisor will have begun to form an impression of you. The appearance of your cover letter and mailing envelope will let him or her know if you are the type of student who takes pride in his or her written work, attends to important details, and understands how to correspond in a professional manner. A well-constructed cover letter is your initial step toward making a good first impression.

Cover letters should be original and confined to one page. Black type on quality white paper (20# bond with at least 25% cotton content) is still the accepted standard. Remember that mass-produced cover letters and random mailings of internship materials are rarely productive. Also, avoid using cover letter "wizards" or modifying one of the countless cover letter examples found online. You want your résumé to stand out. Wizards create similar "looks" and often have programming issues that will affect the cover letter formatting.

The primary considerations in formatting your cover letter are balance and consistency. These two factors, combined with a conventional formal letter layout, result in a cover letter that has "eye appeal" and encourages the recipient to start reading. You might also consider developing a "personal letterhead" for your cover letters. Personal letterheads provide a uniform look to your cover letter and résumé, and the response from agency supervisors has been positive.

All cover letters should correspond to the following points:

1. The amount of white space on the letter is about the same on the top and bottom and the right and left sides.

2. An extra space is used between entries (date and address, paragraphs). Otherwise, single spacing is used.

3. The contact person's full name, title, agency, and address are given.

4. Except in unusual circumstances, the person's formal name (e.g., Mr., Dr., Ms., with his/her last name only) is used, followed by a colon.

5. Three extra spaces are left blank between "Sincerely," and the writer's typed name. The writer's signature (black ink is preferred) goes in this space.

6. The name, present address, and phone (optional) of the writer are given.

7. Use of "Enclosure" lets the reader know that something else is enclosed—in this case, the résumé.

Three slightly different formats of the same cover letter are shown here, one with a personal letterhead and two without personal letterheads. We have added comments to help you identify the unique features of each format. Which one you select is a matter of personal preference; however, no matter which format you prefer, be sure to pay close attention to details (e.g., margin alignment, spacing). Note that each of these letters conforms to all seven of the above points. A completed cover letter must be carefully examined to be sure it conforms to an accepted format and to all points listed above.

SAMPLE LETTER FORMAT #1—BLOCK (WITH LETTERHEAD)

Julie Brown
jbrown222@email.com
2202 Circle Drive
West Coast, CA 95926
(000) 895-5555 (cell)

DATE of Typing — | Date is placed at left margin. |

Mr. Jack Stubler
Director of Recreation
Parkendale Recreation and Parks Department
1011 Duke Drive
Parkendale, CA 00001

| E-mail and address are placed directly below name. Phone number appears below address. |

| First word of each paragraph is *not* indented. |

Dear Mr. Stubler:

I read with interest your article entitled "Creative Financing." I have studied this subject in my courses at West Coast State University, and am currently looking for an internship site that will enhance my understanding of public recreation and creative financing methods.

During my college career, I have had the pleasure to work with many community agencies on various fundraising projects. These experiences have given me the ability to create, develop, and sell ideas and products. Also, I have been elected Northern California Student Representative to the California Park and Recreation Society, Student Branch, and Vice President of the Recreation Student Association at West Coast State University.

Our university's 12-week internship offers me an exciting opportunity to learn from progressive public recreation professionals. Glenda Thomas, a past intern with your agency, indicated that you and your staff could offer me exactly the type of experience I am seeking. Moreover, your promotional brochures and last year's annual report make it clear that the Parkendale Recreation and Parks Department offers innovative programs that are based upon sound management principles. I know that I could learn a great deal from an internship with your agency.

I would like to meet you to discuss further the possibility of our working together. I will call you during the week of April 12 to discuss the possibility of an interview. Thank you for your time and efforts on my behalf.

Sincerely,

Julie Brown

Enclosure: Résumé

SAMPLE LETTER FORMAT #2—BLOCK (WITHOUT LETTERHEAD)

DATE of Typing ————————————— | Date is placed at left margin. |

Mr. Jack Stubler
Director of Recreation
Parkendale Recreation and Parks Department
1011 Duke Drive
Parkendale, CA 00001

| First word of each paragraph is *not* indented. |

Dear Mr. Stubler:

I read with interest your article entitled "Creative Financing." I have studied this subject in my courses at West Coast State University, and am currently looking for an internship site that will enhance my understanding of public recreation and creative financing methods.

During my college career, I have had the pleasure to work with many community agencies on various fundraising projects. These experiences have given me the ability to create, develop, and sell ideas and products. Also, I have been elected Northern California Student Representative to the California Park and Recreation Society, Student Branch, and Vice President of the Recreation Student Association at West Coast State University.

Our university's 12-week internship offers me an exciting opportunity to learn from progressive public recreation professionals. Glenda Thomas, a past intern with your agency, indicated that you and your staff could offer me exactly the type of experience I am seeking. Moreover, your promotional brochures and last year's annual report make it clear that the Parkendale Recreation and Parks Department offers innovative programs that are based upon sound management principles. I know that I could learn a great deal from an internship with your agency.

I would like to meet you to discuss further the possibility of our working together. I will call you during the week of April 12 to discuss the possibility of an interview. Thank you for your time and efforts on my behalf.

Sincerely,

Julie Brown
2202 Circle Drive ————————————— | Address is placed directly below name.
West Coast, CA 95926 | Phone number appears below address. |
(000) 895-5555 (cell)

Enclosure: Résumé

SAMPLE LETTER FORMAT #3—BLOCK (ALTERNATE)

> Address and phone (optional) at top and indented about two thirds across the page for balance.
> **Note**: Name is not given here.

2202 Circle Drive
West Coast, CA 00001
(000) 895-5555

DATE of Typing

Mr. Jack Stubler
Director of Recreation
Parkendale Recreation and Parks Department
1011 Duke Drive
Parkendale, CA 00001

> Rest of letter conforms to same block format as SAMPLE LETTER FORMAT #2.

Dear Mr. Stubler:

I read with interest your article entitled "Creative Financing." I have studied this subject in my courses at West Coast State University, and am currently looking for an internship site that will enhance my understanding of public recreation and creative financing methods.

During my college career, I have had the pleasure to work with many community agencies on various fund-raising projects. These experiences have given me the ability to create, develop, and sell ideas and products. Also, I have been elected Northern California Student Representative to the California Park and Recreation Society, Student Branch, and Vice President of the Recreation Student Association at West Coast State University.

Our university's 12-week internship offers me an exciting opportunity to learn from progressive public recreation professionals. Glenda Thomas, a past intern with your agency, indicated that you and your staff could offer me exactly the type of experience I am seeking. Moreover, your promotional brochures and last year's annual report make it clear that the Parkendale Recreation and Parks Department offers innovative programs that are based upon sound management principles. I know that I could learn a great deal from an internship with your agency.

I would like to meet you to discuss further the possibility of our working together. I will call you during the week of April 12 to discuss the possibility of an interview. Thank you for your time and efforts on my behalf.

Sincerely,

Julie Brown

Enclosure: Résumé

Content of a Cover Letter

The body of a cover letter has four important parts, often addressed in separate paragraphs. The four parts of a well-prepared cover letter include the introduction, connection, personalization, and closing.

Introduction

The first paragraph should let the potential internship supervisor know why you are writing to him or her. This paragraph gives some information, but its primary function is to create a favorable impression, and to let the potential supervisor know that you are interested in an internship with his or her agency. Avoid generic openings such as: "I'm a senior in college…" or "I would like to apply for an internship…" An effective beginning may be to refer to individuals who recommended the agency (e.g., faculty members, professionals), or to explain how you found out about the opportunities offered at the agency (e.g., newspaper advertisements, notices in journals). Referring to such information shows the employer you have taken the time to gather your facts. This paragraph should also indicate that you are interested in the *possibility* of doing an internship with the agency, and provide information on the length (or dates) of the internship.

Connection

This paragraph of the cover letter describes to the prospective internship supervisor your knowledge of the agency, and how your skills and career interests match the agency's needs. Briefly summarize important aspects of your résumé, plus any other information that may not appear in the résumé (e.g., specific courses you have taken). The main purpose of the connection paragraph is to convince the prospective supervisor that you have skills that will benefit the agency during your internship.

Personalization

You not only want a prospective internship supervisor to know you are qualified to be an intern, but you also want him or her to know you hope to learn a great deal from your internship experience. The third paragraph allows you to personalize; thus, you let the potential supervisor know what it is about the agency that is important to you. What are they doing that you want to be a part of? What unique learning experiences do they offer? This information can only be obtained by researching the company (see Chapter Three).

Note: Many students and professionals prefer to combine the *connection* and *personalization* aspects into a single paragraph. Some examples of three-paragraph cover letters are included in this chapter.

Closing

The final paragraph answers the question, "What happens next?" You need to let the prospective internship supervisor know that you plan to follow up by phone to discuss the possibility of doing an internship with his or her agency. Do *not* wait to be contacted by the agency! Also let him or her know that you would appreciate a personal interview. Do not demand an interview—the prospective supervisor should control future meetings. If the distance is too great for you to visit the agency, request a telephone interview. Finally, you should express your appreciation to the prospective supervisor.

With a cover letter (and résumé, too), it's not only *what* you say, but *how* you say it that counts. Potential internship supervisors are looking for students who attend to details and avoid errors in their work. You can demonstrate this in your cover letter by using correct grammar and avoiding spelling and typographical errors. In general, you should also avoid using abbreviations, acronyms, and contractions. To send the best possible cover letter, we urge you to type each letter individually using a computer with laser printer and:

- Put the completed letter aside for at least 24 hours, then carefully reread it at least four times
- When you think it is perfect, give it to a *knowledgeable* friend or relative to read for comprehension, grammar, and spelling

- *Always* use a computer spell-checking program prior to final printing of your cover letter. Do not depend exclusively upon this, however (see box below)

When a Computerized Spell Check Fails

Computer spell checking software is a valuable tool, but it cannot take the place of careful proofreading. Spell checkers only identify words that are misspelled; therefore, they do not identify the *wrong* word that is spelled correctly. The following humorous mistakes were actually submitted by students. They may have used spell checkers, but they did *not* proofread.

My work as a camp counselor has helped me gain valuable experience in ants and crafts.
While working at my present job, I have served as a leader for sex groups of adults.
I also have sigh language skills.
I enjoy being in the presents of other people.
This exorcise helped me to understand how to work better with others.
I have worked hard to create a homely environment for participants.
My day damp experiences have helped me to understand the needs of children.
I have used my sign language skills to serve as an interrupter for a person who is deaf.

Final Tips and Reminders about the Cover Letter

1. Be sure to address your letter to a specific person, and include his or her job title. Double-check the spelling of the person's name prior to mailing.

2. Follow up by phone within one week of the letter's arrival to discuss the possibility of an interview.

3. Use high-quality paper that is identical to your résumé. We suggest 20# bond with at least 25% cotton content.

4. Use a high quality envelope to mail your cover letter and résumé, and make sure that it is addressed properly (typed and free from spelling errors). If possible, have the envelope match the paper you are using for the cover letter and résumé. Remember, a good first impression is vital, and the first thing a potential internship supervisor sees is your envelope.

Exercise Time

Exercise 4.1 intends to help you to identify errors in both format and content in a cover letter. At this point, test your understanding of cover letters by circling the errors and missing information in Exercise 4.1 and then turn the page for the answers.

Exercise 4.1: Find Errors and Omissions

Sally Doe
sjd100@email.com
111 Cherry Street
East Coast, PA 10001
(000) 891-0000 (cell)

September 3, 2012

Ms. Anna E. Bell
Mapac, Inc.
1205 Baker Street, Suite 120
State College, PA 00001

Dear Anna Bell,

Since our discussion on August 19th, I have had the oppurtunity to meet with Dr. Joseph Bright, my internship coordinator. He agreed with me that completing an internship with Mapac in the Department of Public Relations would be an excellent learning experience. I look forward to the possibility of contributing my creativity and knowledge of public relations to your organization.

Currently, I am finishing my capstone courses at East Coast State University in both my business and communication majors. I am especially excited about my business law and international communication classes. Both of these courses are teaching me practical skills that will help me contribute to your department and assist me in my professional growth.

I will be in State College on September 27th, and would appreciate it if we could get together to discuss my doing an internship with Mapac. I will call you during the week of September 16th to establish a time for our meeting.

Sincerely,

Sally Doe

Answers to Exercise 4.1

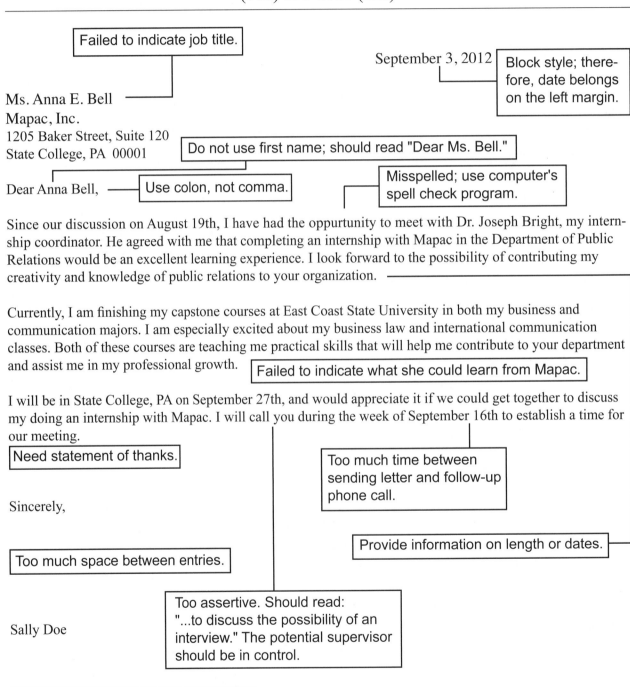

Sally Doe
sjd100@email.com
111 Cherry Street
East Coast, PA 10001
(000) 891-0000 (cell)

September 3, 2012

Block style; therefore, date belongs on the left margin.

Failed to indicate job title.

Ms. Anna E. Bell
Mapac, Inc.
1205 Baker Street, Suite 120
State College, PA 00001

Do not use first name; should read "Dear Ms. Bell."

Dear Anna Bell,

Use colon, not comma.

Misspelled; use computer's spell check program.

Since our discussion on August 19th, I have had the oppurtunity to meet with Dr. Joseph Bright, my internship coordinator. He agreed with me that completing an internship with Mapac in the Department of Public Relations would be an excellent learning experience. I look forward to the possibility of contributing my creativity and knowledge of public relations to your organization.

Currently, I am finishing my capstone courses at East Coast State University in both my business and communication majors. I am especially excited about my business law and international communication classes. Both of these courses are teaching me practical skills that will help me contribute to your department and assist me in my professional growth.

Failed to indicate what she could learn from Mapac.

I will be in State College, PA on September 27th, and would appreciate it if we could get together to discuss my doing an internship with Mapac. I will call you during the week of September 16th to establish a time for our meeting.

Need statement of thanks.

Too much time between sending letter and follow-up phone call.

Sincerely,

Provide information on length or dates.

Too much space between entries.

Too assertive. Should read: "...to discuss the possibility of an interview." The potential supervisor should be in control.

Sally Doe

Need to indicate résumé is enclosed.

Sample Cover Letters

Carefully review the cover letters provided. They are good examples of letters that may help you. Use them for guidance, but be sure to write *your* letter in your own style and wording. Note that some of these letters may deviate slightly from the content guidelines given above. It is not essential that your letters conform *exactly* to our content guidelines, but it is important that all necessary information is included in a neat, well-formatted, and error-free cover letter.

Note that cover letters #2 through #5 use a personal letterhead approach. All businesses have some form of letterhead that clearly identifies their business to correspondents. You might consider developing your own personal letterhead that identifies you and helps your cover letter stand out to prospective internship site supervisors. This approach also enables you to provide a uniform look to your cover letter and résumé. Also, cover letters should open with an exciting and directed paragraph. See the next page for examples.

Cover Letters (Opening Paragraph Examples)

I have enjoyed working at Ronald McDonald Camp for children with special needs during the past summer. The recreation program has enhanced my credibility as a recreation professional. I am in my last semester at Bloomsburg State University and am currently looking for an internship site that will assist me in utilizing the recreation skills which I have acquired.

My academic advisor suggested I contact you regarding the possibilities of an internship. Having lived in the area for 15 years, I am very familiar with the local area, climate, and many scenic attractions. I would like to explore the possibility of completing an internship with your agency.

I have been researching various agencies and my thoughts keep coming back to how impressed I was with your agency's programs and services. In March, I talked to you about your internship program. I was able to tour the facilities and get an understanding of what would be required in an internship.

Have you ever looked out into the crowd while giving a talk and seen the look of wonder on a visitor's face, that gleam in a child's eyes, or heard that "gasp" of realization? The exhilaration of being an interpreter and sharing with visitors the incredible diversity and wonder of nature can be one of the most beneficial rewards of the job.

I recently read about your innovative recreation programs, and am excited about the learning opportunities your agency could offer me. Beginning in September, I will participate in an internship program as part of my academic career. After receiving information on your facilities, I realized your programs correspond with my professional career goals. I would like to explore an internship option with your agency.

After our discussion, I am excited to learn more about your program. I am interested in working at Hopland Rehabilitation Hospital because I would like to work in a clinical setting. I would like to experience a clinical setting doing assessment, documentation, charting, evaluation, and work with other allied professionals. Physical rehabilitation is an area I would like to work in after graduation; therefore, your program corresponds with my professional interests.

SAMPLE COVER LETTER #1

DATE of Typing

Ms. Anna E. Bell
Director of Public Relations
Mapac, Inc.
1205 Baker Street, Suite 120
State College, CA 94001

Dear Ms. Bell:

Since our discussion on (DATE), I have had the opportunity to meet with Dr. Joseph Bright, my internship coordinator. He agreed with me that completing an internship with Mapac in the Department of Public Relations would be an excellent learning experience. For spring semester, our 15-week (full-time) internship begins on January 20th and ends on May 2nd. I look forward to the possibility of contributing my creativity and knowledge of public relations to your organization.

Currently, I am finishing my capstone courses at East Coast State University in both my business and communication majors. I am especially enthusiastic about my business law and international communication classes. Both of these courses are teaching me practical skills that will help me contribute to your department and assist me in my professional growth.

Working with your department would give me an understanding of the requirements of an entry-level position at Mapac. In addition, it would offer me the opportunity to work with knowledgeable professionals, and to integrate classroom theory and practical experience. I am very excited about the possibility of working with you.

I will be in State College on (DATE), and would appreciate it if we could get together to discuss my doing an internship with Mapac. I will call you during the week of (DATE) to discuss the possibility of an interview. Thank you for your interest and your time.

Sincerely,

Sally Doe
111 Cherry Street
East Coast, PA 10001
(916) 000-2222

Enclosure: Résumé

Examples of Personal Letterheads

All businesses have some form of business letterhead to help customers identify them. Why not take that same idea for students seeking internships? Our students have used this idea for a few years and the response from businesses and agencies has been positive. It is easy and provides a uniform look to your cover letter and résumé. Some examples of cover letters using personal letterheads are presented below. Be creative; however, be professional in what you present to prospective internship supervisors.

KIMBERLY RICKETTS
kricketts245@email.com

Local Address	*Permanent Address*
100 Brook Drive	333 Mission Drive
San Antonio, TX 95926	Dallas, TX 95817
530-898-6666	916-451-3000

Kimberly Ricketts
kricketts245@email.com
100 Brook Drive
San Antonio, TX 95926
530-898-6666
530-891-4444 (cell)

KIMBERLY RICKETTS
kricketts245@email.com
100 Brook Drive
San Antonio, TX 95926
530-898-6666
530-891-4444 (cell)

Kimberly Ricketts
✉100 Brook Dr., San Antonio, TX 95926 ☎530-891-4444 (cell)
kricketts245@email.com

These were easily created by using Microsoft Word. Once the table is created, go to Border and Shading and block out some of the lines or make the lines bolder. See examples on the following pages and determine for yourself if you like the format.

SAMPLE COVER LETTER #2

Teri Sampson
tsampson@email.com
530-891-5555 (cell)

Local Address	**Permanent Address**
120 Beach Street	111 San Pablo Street
Tampa, FL 95926	Durham, NC 95817
530-899-8000	916-345-9000

DATE of Typing

Janelle Fonda
The Pacific Coast Baseball League
1200 Baseball Drive
Bend, OR 93333

Dear Ms. Fonda:

I have always been excited about athletics and sporting events. As I finish my career as a Special Events major, I want to move into a direction that keeps me around sporting events. I am currently looking for an internship or work experience in which I can pursue my passion for planning events and providing excellent customer service. Your league has a wonderful reputation for both and I would like to join your special events team.

I have seen The Pacific Coast Baseball League organization grow in success and make a difference in the communities it is involved with. It is exceptional how you plan your events over the course of a season and I would like to be a part of that. Also, from your website, I have observed the many special events each team performs in its community, from cancer walks, Habitat for Humanity building, and lunches for people who are homeless. How to plan these programs is what my education centered upon, and I believe I would like to help your team as it performs excellent community services.

During my college career, I played four years of varsity softball. In between my practices, I studied event planning as well as community and commercial recreation administration. During my time in college, I got to experience many different events including organizing fundraisers and tournaments. In my classes, I have been able to be part of all areas of event planning and budgeting. I have also spent my last two summers working with the Miami Wave, an independent baseball league learning the ins and outs of their operations.

I would like to meet with you to see if I would be a good fit in your organization. I will call you in two weeks to see if I may schedule an interview with you. Thank you for your time.

Sincerely,

Teri Sampson

Enclosure: Résumé

SAMPLE COVER LETTER #3

Thomas Jones
tjones12@email.com
899 Nord Avenue
Chico, CA 95926
530-332-1666 (cell)

DATE of typing

Bob Little, Senior Vice President
OSI Restaurant Partners, Inc.
22222 North West Shore Boulevard
Jacksonville, FL 33607

Dear Mr. Little:

I have been in the Food and Beverage business for about five years. In that time, I have worked as a caterer, baker, cook, server, and bartender. Currently, I am majoring in Resort and Lodging Management and want to continue my career in the food and beverage industry. I am seeking an internship as a management trainee with your organization because I have found that the best way to get into this field is to actually work with someone who does just that. I chose your organization because of the professionalism that your employees exhibit and the positive reputation of your company.

Going back to my experience in the field of food and beverage management, some of the skills that I have picked up are communication skills with Hispanic employees, customer satisfaction, preparation skills, cleanliness, purchasing, and I also have experienced working with large equipment in big kitchens. Skills that I have gained in school that are useful to your organization are budgeting, team leadership, cost control, employment laws, and I also have some knowledge in wine paring. I think the skills that I possess are a true benefit to your organization because this is a field that is always changing in terms of what customers want and I enjoy the challenge.

I will contact you before the end of the month to discuss a time for a possible meeting. Please review my attached résumé for further information. Thank you so much for your time, and I look forward to talking with you and discussing the possibility of an internship with your company.

Sincerely,

Thomas Jones

Enclosure: Résumé

SAMPLE COVER LETTER #4

William Steel

1111 Hazel Avenue, Normal, IL 92815   <u>wsteel006@hotmail.com</u>   (562) 985-1000

DATE of typing

Steven Neal
Recreation Therapist
Los Angeles County Mental Health Treatment Center
333 Long Beach Blvd.
Los Angeles, CA 92815

Dear Mr. Neal:

Sally Smith, Internship Coordinator at Midwestern State University, has encouraged me to contact you concerning a position as Intern in your Recreational Therapy department. After reviewing your packet and visiting your facility, I am confident that your team and facility would provide me with an excellent experience in Recreational Therapy.

During my college career, I have worked with a variety of populations. Throughout those experiences, I have been fascinated with mental illness. Some of those experiences include working with individuals who have: been sexually and physically abused, depression, schizophrenia, and Alzheimer's disease. Due to these experiences, I want to focus my career on working with individuals diagnosed with mental illness. I am equally comfortable working independently or as part of a team and am highly motivated to learn.

Academically, I am in the top 15% of my class, and in the top 10% of Recreation majors. As my volunteer and work experiences attest, I am dedicated to the Therapeutic Recreation field. I am also a member of the Midwestern Parks and Recreation Society (MPRS), Golden Key Honor Society, and the Illinois Response Team. Please review my enclosed résumé for further details.

An internship with your agency would give me an opportunity to learn from my future peers, and help to ensure that I will be successful in my future. I would appreciate a personal interview and will contact you soon to discuss further the possibility of our working together.

Thank you for your time and consideration.

Sincerely,

William Steel

Enclosure: Résumé

SAMPLE COVER LETTER #5

JACKIE GREEN
jgreen132@email.com

Local Address	*Permanent Address*
100 Brook Drive	333 Mission Drive
Boston, MA 63801	Boston, MA 63803
730-898-6666	730-451-3000

DATE of typing

Mr. Robert Saunders
Manager/Owner
Fitness For Life
400 Martin Avenue
University City, PA 16755

Dear Mr. Saunders:

After many years of athletic involvement through competitive swimming and running, I am eager to start my career in the fitness industry. Through my university's career file, I have learned that your agency has previously accepted Northeast State University students for their internship experiences. Please consider me a candidate for an internship with your organization during the coming fall semester. Enclosed is my résumé for your review. Our full-time internship begins on September 2nd and ends on December 13th.

I have been a member of your club since (date of membership), and have a general understanding of the facility and its operations. My athletic experience has given me the opportunity to visit and utilize a variety of facilities, and I have worked with people of all ages and physical abilities. Through my internship, I would like to learn more about your agency's operation, especially the areas of marketing and advertising. Northeast's internship is 12 weeks in length and 40 hours per week. I believe that Fitness For Life can add to my college experience and give me a better understanding of the industry I am preparing to enter.

I would appreciate the opportunity to discuss my internship with you in further detail. I will call you at your office the week of (specify week) to discuss the possibility of an interview. Thank you for your time.

Sincerely,

Jackie Green

Enclosure: Résumé

Summary

This chapter has provided information, exercises, and examples for writing your cover letter. It emphasized the importance of a well-prepared cover letter, including attention to both content and format. The cover letter does not stand alone, however. It introduces you to a prospective internship supervisor and highlights your résumé, which accompanies the cover letter. Together, a quality cover letter and résumé will increase your chances of getting the internship you desire.

Now it is time to begin preparing your résumé. The next chapter will provide you with information on creating a professional résumé that attracts and holds the attention of a potential internship supervisor. Like Chapter Four, the next chapter will also provide exercises and examples to help you. The end result will be a résumé you can distribute with pride.

Chapter Five
Preparation: The Résumé

Nothing which has entered into our experience is ever lost.—William Ellery Channing

No written document is more important to your internship plans than your résumé, and few documents take more time and effort to prepare. This chapter will help you to develop your professional résumé, with special attention to the "little" things that will make your résumé stand out. This chapter will also provide you with examples of résumés that have proven effective in securing internships in recreation and leisure services.

To construct the best possible résumé, you need to:
- Develop a "foundation" or "working" résumé
- Know what a "professional" résumé is, including acceptable formats and appropriate content
- Select your references
- Review examples of résumés
- Consider developing a portfolio

Your résumé is more than a written summary of your experiences, skills, achievements, and interests—it is your own personal marketing device. It provides you with an opportunity to sell yourself to a potential internship agency, and like the cover letter it offers a chance to demonstrate your professional writing skills to a potential internship supervisor. A well-organized, attractive, and informative résumé not only helps you to secure the best possible internship, but also proves invaluable when you prepare your employment résumé prior to graduation.

Will a good résumé get you the internship you seek? Probably not, but a bad one certainly can *lose* it for you. A poorly constructed, inconsistent, or error-filled résumé may result in being eliminated from consideration without an interview. A properly prepared résumé, however, will attract the reader's attention and go a long way toward securing the interview you need.

Unfortunately, there is no magical formula for preparing the "perfect" résumé. Each potential internship supervisor has his or her own personal preferences regarding the format and content of a résumé. Nevertheless, there are a lot of things you can do to ensure that your résumé is complete and appeals to the maximum number of professionals in recreation and leisure services. The information in this chapter is based upon a wide variety of written sources, plus many conversations with internship supervisors. It intends to help you to prepare the best possible résumé—a résumé that will open the interview doors for the internship that *you* want.

The "Foundation" or "Working" Résumé

To build your résumé we suggest you create two documents containing information for your use. First, construct what we call a "foundation" (or "working") résumé. This document will contain everything there is to know about you. Just write down everything that you think might be important—that is, all education, work experiences (paid/volunteer), achievements, certificates, workshops and seminars attended, hobbies/recreational pursuits, and potential references. Do not worry about the format. Just put information down. Some of this information may seem irrelevant; however, experience teaches us there may be times when you will use this information. It is always better to be prepared.

Exercise Time

 To help you, we have included a Foundation Résumé Worksheet (Exercise 5.1). Use this worksheet to list all information about yourself that might be useful to a prospective internship supervisor. Later, you can use this foundation résumé to pick and choose any combination of information or facts that meet the criteria for the specific internship (or employment) position you are seeking. After you select the information you need, you can begin to polish the content in preparation for your "professional" résumé.

Exercise 5.1: Foundation Résumé Worksheet

Name, Address, Phone numbers, E-mail (local and permanent)

_____

_____

_____

_____

Career Objective (optional)

_____

_____

_____

_____

Skills/Accomplishments (be specific)

_____

_____

_____

_____

Education

_____

_____

_____

_____

Workshops/Seminars Attended

_____

_____

_____

_____

_____

Work (Business) Experience

_____

_____

_____

_____

_____

Work (Volunteer or Extracurricular) Experience

_____

_____

_____

_____

_____

Awards, Honors, Certificates

_____

_____

_____

_____

_____

Memberships

_____

_____

_____

_____

_____

References (include title or position, addresses, phone numbers, e-mails)

_____

_____

_____

_____

_____

Interest and Hobbies (related to internship)

_____

_____

_____

_____

_____

Other Pertinent Information

_____

_____

_____

_____

_____

The "Professional" Résumé

The second document is the typical résumé used by professionals—the one that most people think of when they hear the word "résumé." It is the one-page or two-page résumé that you will use the majority of the time. Most students at the entry level only need a one-page résumé; however, students with extensive professional experience may find a two-page résumé more appropriate. If you are looking for an internship in a commercial business where you may be competing with students from marketing, business, public relations, etc., plan to develop a one-page résumé.

Most experts suggest using either a *chronological résumé*, which lists specific experiences in order by dates, or a *functional résumé*, which documents skills, knowledge, abilities, and accomplishments without emphasizing dates. The functional résumé is better for the person who has been out of the job market for an extended period of time, or has gaps between experiences that are difficult to explain. *Electronic* and *scannable* résumés are increasingly used to screen job applicants, particularly when the pool of potential applicants is large. Some of the online resources provided in Appendix A have résumé services offering electronic résumé submission. These résumés are rarely used for internships, however; nor are they commonly used by recreation and leisure agencies.

Generally, students and professionals in recreation and leisure services prefer to use the chronological résumé. Therefore, this chapter emphasizes the chronological résumé. We do, however, suggest you consider adding a section to your chronological résumé that lists specific skills. If you believe a functional résumé is best for you, consult the recommended readings listed in Appendix C. Information on the format and content of electronic and scannable résumés is included at the end of this chapter.

Format and Content of the Print Résumé

Your résumé is your personal marketing device. It is essential that it be:

1. *Professional in Appearance.* Your résumé should be prepared on a computer and printed on a high-quality printer. This will provide a professional appearance *and* make subsequent revisions much easier. If possible, individually print each résumé. If you decide to make copies, be sure they are *exceptionally* high in quality. Print (or copy) your résumé on the same quality paper as your cover letter (20# bond with at least 25% cotton content). With respect to color, research indicates that most professionals in recreation and leisure studies prefer white, off-white, cream, or beige paper.

   Note: If you are going to have your résumé prepared and/or printed by a commercial company, it is still your responsibility to have the information ready and in the format you desire.

2. *Clear and Concise.* Your résumé should be simple and easy to read. Use words and expressions that are easily understood and express precisely what you want to say. Avoid jargon. Edit your professional résumé unmercifully. Eliminate unnecessary words and phrases. Be certain that every piece of information is important and stated as briefly as possible (without violating rule #3).

3. *Thorough.* Be sure that all relevant information is included. If you are listing items chronologically, do not leave gaps of time that are unexplained. If necessary, your cover letter should be used to explain gaps. Also, be sure to document all important tasks or learning opportunities associated with a given experience. Use action verbs to demonstrate your capabilities. A list of action verbs is provided later in this chapter (see Resource #1, p. 101).

4. *Error-Free.* Use every possible means to eliminate errors. Use the computer's spell checking software. *Slowly* proofread the résumé. Also, ask a friend or relative who is proficient in English grammar to proofread your résumé. The importance of proofreading cannot be overemphasized. One poll, cited by On the Mark Media, found that "84 percent of executives say it takes just one typographical error in a résumé for them to remove a candidate from job consideration" (*Centre Daily Times,* February 18, 2007, p. D9).

5. *Balanced and Consistent.* Your résumé should be balanced on the page. Too much writing on one side, top or bottom, can make the résumé appear "lopsided." White spaces (areas not containing text) should also be balanced throughout the résumé. Careful attention should be paid to consistency of

margins and indentions (e.g., identical margins for headings, uniform indentions within sections). Consistency in wording is important, too.

6. *The Truth.* The information in your résumé should make you look as good as possible, but *not* at the expense of the truth. *Never* lie on a résumé, overstate your accomplishments, or mislead a potential internship supervisor regarding your experiences or responsibilities. Be selective in what you include in your résumé, but be sure it is the truth.

In addition to the essential information, there are many things to keep in mind when preparing a print résumé. Some of the more important ones include:

1. Readers pay the *most* attention to the beginning of a page, paragraph, sentence, or list. Therefore, be sure to structure your résumé to

   a. Get the most important sections (e.g., profile statements, professional experiences) toward the beginning of the résumé.

   b. List experiences beginning with the most recent, working back to those in the past.

   c. Give the most relevant responsibilities or skills first.

2. Do not put personal information such as sex, height, weight, age, or marital status in your résumé.

3. Provide brief descriptions of your professional (and other) work experiences that show skills. Consider using profile statements to summarize your professional attributes. Use action verbs.

4. Make sure words in a series are in the same tense and form. Only use present tense if you are still involved in an activity or work experience. Avoid personal pronouns (e.g., I, me, he, she).

5. Do not use abbreviations/acronyms by themselves, unless they are *universally* known and accepted (e.g., EMT, CPR, postal abbreviations for states). Thus, NRPA should be listed: National Recreation and Park Association (NRPA). In general, contractions should be avoided as well.

6. Highlight headings and important information by using boldface type, italics, or underlining. These techniques add emphasis and are important to maintaining good balance on the page.

7. *Never* print (or copy) a two-page résumé back-to-back. Staple (or paper-clip) the pages together in the upper left-hand corner, and be sure to include your name on page two. Also, make sure the text extends *at least* halfway down page two. If not, expand the text or reduce the résumé to one page.

8. Do not put a page break in the middle of an entry. Also, try to avoid splitting a section (e.g., professional experience) between pages. If you do split a section, be sure to put the heading with "Continued" specified on page two. "Cont'd" is also acceptable, even though it is a contraction.

9. If possible, references should be included on the résumé, and they should be the last item. If they are listed on a separate sheet of paper, it is not necessary to refer to them on the résumé.

Select your references with care, keeping the prospective internship agency and supervisor in mind. Three or four references should be provided, but you should also identify one or two others that you do not put down in writing. Thus, you will be prepared if an interviewer asks you for additional references not included on your printed list. If possible, your reference list should include past or present employers, educators, or established adults who know your personal character (e.g., parent of a friend, member of the clergy, recreation leader). Always ask for permission before including anyone on your reference list.

The rules for preparing your reference list are the same as the rules for your résumé and cover letter (i.e., professional appearance, well-balanced on page, high-quality paper). Each reference should be printed or typed in block form and include the person's full name, title (if appropriate), complete mailing address, and phone number. If the person has a fax number and e-mail address, include them also. Generally, a work address is preferred because most reference checks are done during the workday.

Profile Statements

Profile statements are sometimes used near the beginning of a print résumé to summarize and emphasize the applicant's most positive attributes. If you decide to use profile statements, no more than five statements should be listed; moreover, all statements must be *completely* accurate descriptions of your capabilities. Following are some potential profile statements. During an interview, be prepared to support your statements with specific examples of "how" you have demonstrated these skills:

- Strong interpersonal and communication skills
- Extensive experience in design and implementation of adventure programs
- Calm and work well under demanding conditions
- Strong commitment to the needs and interests of clients
- Proven management skills and record of accomplishments
- Highly skilled in effective outdoor leadership techniques
- Experience and training in numerous computer software packages
- Skilled supervisor, with ability to motivate others and handle conflict effectively
- Creative and flexible in organizing, planning and leading therapeutic activities
- Good eye for detail; well-organized and skilled in marketing programs
- Strong problem-solving skills
- Effective in promoting a positive, productive work environment
- Skilled in accurately assessing needs and developing program criteria
- Dependable and hard working; get along well with clients and colleagues
- Wide variety of outdoor recreation-related skills and interests
- Well-organized; strong in planning and implementing programs
- Effectively work with persons from diverse backgrounds
- Enthusiastic, high energy, and creative in program development
- Positive, professional attitude; committed to excellence
- Outstanding oral presentation skills
- Strength in innovative program planning and evaluation
- Special talent for training and motivating volunteer staff
- Coordinated highly successful special events
- Infectious enthusiasm for promoting programs
- Proven record of success in leading experiential education activities
- Talent for getting diverse groups to work well together
- Ability to prioritize, delegate, and motivate
- Able to pull together and manage all aspects of a complex project
- Reputation for taking the initiative and seeing a task through to completion
- Skilled in handling the public with professionalism and sensitivity
- Establish excellent relations with customers; build loyal repeat business
- Sharp, innovative, quick learner; proven ability to adapt quickly to change
- Communicate easily with a wide range of personalities
- Able to meet deadlines and work with minimal supervision

Commercial Résumé Preparation and Printing

If you do not have good computer skills, you may decide to use a commercial résumé service or printing firm. Here are some tips about having your materials commercially prepared:

1. Check out the commercial service or printer first. Ask to see résumés they have printed for other people (most printers keep copies of résumés they produce).

2. Check out the service or printer's prices (e.g., preparation estimates, printing, quality of paper, paper colors, quantity price, ability to make simple changes).

3. The service or printer should provide you with a proof for your review. When you receive the proof, make certain you check it over (at least four times) for misspelled words or other errors. Have others check it, too. Printers will not usually change a résumé once it is printed if *you* missed a mistake. Once you initial the proof for printing, the responsibility for errors has shifted to you and not the printer.

4. Remember to check your completed résumé before you leave the service or printer's place of business. Is the format proper? Is the print dark? Is the quality of paper what you specified?

5. ***Important:*** Make certain the service or printer does not reproduce your résumé from an "assembly line" approach. You don't want your résumé to look like everyone else's. Printers must respect your wishes because it is your money you are spending. Be assertive. Make sure you get the résumé you want.

Preparing Your Résumé

The pages that follow intend to help you to prepare your own résumé. Resource #1 gives a list of action verbs—the type of words that should be used in a résumé. Resource #2 offers a Résumé Guide to assist you. Once you have completed a draft of your résumé, use the Résumé Checklist (Resource #3) to ensure that your résumé conforms to the suggestions in this manual.

In preparing your résumé, you should refer to the many examples included in the next section of this chapter; however, remember that your résumé is a reflection of you. Construct your résumé using your own wording, and select a format, font, and style that presents a professional image. To avoid your résumé looking like everyone else's, you should not use a computer résumé template. The result should be a résumé you are proud of—and one that gets you the internship interview you want.

RESOURCE #1—ACTION VERBS FOR USE IN PRINT RÉSUMÉS

Below is a list of action verbs that indicate to a prospective internship supervisor (or employer) you are a person who gets things done. Also, using a variety of these verbs in your résumé demonstrates diverse skills, knowledge, and abilities. Circle those you want to include in your résumé. Pay particular attention to verbs critical to success in your area of specialization. You may also want to add some verbs of your own.

Accomplished	Edited	Performed
Achieved	Educated	Planned
Adapted	Eliminated	Prepared
Administered	Employed	Presented
Advanced	Enforced	Processed
Advocated	Established	Procured
Advised	Evaluated	Produced
Analyzed	Expanded	Programmed
Applied	Expedited	Promoted
Appointed	Formed	Proposed
Arranged	Founded	Provided
Assessed	Fulfilled	Published
Assigned	Generated	Purchased
Assisted	Guided	Recommended
Authored	Handled	Redesigned
Broadened	Hired	Reduced
Built	Identified	Reorganized
Centralized	Implemented	Represented
Charted	Improved	Researched
Clarified	Increased	Resolved
Coached	Influenced	Restored
Collaborated	Initiated	Restructured
Collected	Installed	Reviewed
Completed	Instigated	Revised
Composed	Instituted	Saved
Conceived	Instructed	Scheduled
Conceptualized	Integrated	Secured
Conducted	Interpreted	Selected
Conserved	Interviewed	Served
Consulted	Introduced	Sold
Contracted	Inventoried	Solved
Contributed	Investigated	Specified
Controlled	Launched	Strengthened
Coordinated	Led	Structured
Counseled	Located	Studied
Created	Maintained	Suggested
Decreased	Managed	Supervised
Delivered	Marketed	Taught
Demonstrated	Modified	Tested
Designed	Monitored	Trained
Determined	Negotiated	Undertook
Developed	Obtained	Utilized
Directed	Operated	Won
Discovered	Ordered	Wrote
Distributed	Organized	
Documented	Participated	

RESOURCE #2—RÉSUMÉ GUIDE

1. *Heading:* Name, current address, home and cell phones. If your current address is temporary, you may want to list your permanent address as well.

2. *Career objective* (optional): This can be covered more extensively in your cover letter, and including it may limit the use of your résumé. Most agencies assume that you have tailored your objective to the specific internship for which you are applying and, thus, your objective may not have much value. If you need more room on your résumé, you might consider deleting your objective and using the space for more important information.

3. *Education* (e.g., community college, college, university): Generally, high school should not be listed. *Optional:* You may also want to put a list of courses you have taken that are relevant to your major and specialization.

4. *Computer skills* (optional): Include working knowledge of software (e.g., Excel, Word, PowerPoint).

5. *Work and/or volunteer experience*: This category is often divided into two sections (e.g., paid and volunteer, professional and other work). Dividing this category may help you get the most important experiences at the beginning of a section. However, do not divide the category if a section is limited to only one experience. Describe the experience according to the skills that you demonstrated in the position. Use action verbs to create action phrases. Make the experiences sound like they belong to you—that you actually did them and did them well.

    Many times, students are faced with the fact that they have more professionally related volunteer experience than paid work experience. In this case, it might be more effective to label your categories differently. For example, instead of using "Work Experience" and "Volunteer Experience," you might use "Professional Experience" (include work and volunteer professional experience) and "Related Experience" (include work and volunteer related experience). By taking this approach, all of your professionally related experience will appear at the top of your résumé.

6. *Skill areas/accomplishments* (optional): An easy-to-read listing of your skills and accomplishments may be useful to emphasize your abilities. This can be an important area, especially if your work and/or volunteer history is limited. Profession-related service may also be listed here.

7. *Awards, honors, certificates, licenses*: Remember not to abbreviate or use acronyms. List the entire title, with the abbreviated title in parentheses.

8. *Memberships* (community/campus organizations, professional associations): Be sure to list offices held and responsibilities.

9. *Interests and hobbies:* Some companies like to see that their employees have interests away from work; it demonstrates a balance of life. Also, this section can show you have skills important to a recreation/leisure service professional.

10. *References:* Include references on the résumé or submit them on a separate sheet enclosed with your résumé. If they are listed on a separate sheet and included with the résumé, it is not necessary to refer to them on the résumé. You should avoid using "References available upon request." For additional information on references, see page 136.

Note: The order of categories #3 through #7 is sometimes changed, depending upon what the applicant wants to emphasize. Most professionals expect to see education first, however.

RESOURCE #3—RÉSUMÉ CHECKLIST

_____ Material fits neatly on one or two pages. If two pages, at least half of the second page is filled with text. Also, the top of page two includes name and the text begins with a new entry.

_____ Overall appearance is balanced (both pages, if two-page résumé), including adequate white space at top, bottom, sides, and between entries.

_____ No spelling, grammatical, or punctuation errors.

_____ Printing or typing is neat, clean, and looks professional.

_____ Name, address(es), and telephone number(s) are at the top.

_____ Writing style is concise and direct. Information is easy to read.

_____ Abbreviations or acronyms, if used, are in parentheses and preceded by full title. Contractions and personal pronouns (e.g., I, me, my) are not used.

_____ Paragraph information is brief, to the point, and complete.

_____ Words in a series are in the same tense and form.

_____ All appropriate education, work experiences, skills, and other information are included in the résumé.

_____ Important titles are emphasized by bold print or underlined, where appropriate, but these techniques are not overused.

_____ Indentions are appropriately used to set off information and create eye appeal and uniform within sections.

_____ Accomplishments and experiences are described using action verbs to create action phrases.

_____ Dates are uniform, with no big gaps.

_____ Personal data (e.g., sex, height, age, marital status) are not included.

_____ Overall résumé demonstrates your ability to produce results.

Also have other people check your résumé using this checklist.

Sample Print Résumés

The following pages provide examples of well-prepared chronological résumés. We begin with a simple straightforward résumé format and move to more complex formats for your review. Both one-page and two-page résumés are included. These résumés are presented as examples only. As mentioned earlier, *there is no absolutely perfect résumé format*. Look these résumés over, paying careful attention to both *what* is included and *how* it is presented. We have added comments on some résumés to highlight important aspects. Do not only look at the comments, however. Examine each résumé thoroughly. Determine what aspects you want to use for your own résumé. We have tried to include résumés representing a variety of specializations within the recreation and leisure profession.

The résumés in this manual were done inexpensively because they were prepared on a computer; however, they did take considerable time to construct. You can stay away from expensive commercial résumé preparation costs if you have access to a computer with word processing or desktop publishing software. The résumés in this manual were constructed using InDesign/PageMaker or Microsoft Word software.

When looking at the different formats in our examples, notice the bold lines, lines used to separate information, and use of other techniques to emphasize specific information. These techniques add emphasis and style to the print résumé; however, be careful not to overuse such devices. If a résumé is considered too "flashy" it may result in a rejection letter.

Note: The two examples of print résumés on pages 117–120 (#8 and #9) demonstrate an innovative way to combine your cover letter and résumé into a one-page, three-fold document. This unique cover letter/résumé might excite potential internship supervisors, especially in the special event, outdoor guide, or entertainment industries.

SAMPLE PRINT RÉSUMÉ #1

Michael Smith
100 North Cherry Street
Manaugua, Minnesota 55800
(000) 894-0000

> Note balance and effective use of white space.

Education

Minnesota State University at Manaugua
Bachelor of Arts, Recreation Administration: Graduation (DATE)
Option: Resort and Lodging Management
Minor: Business Administration
3.80 overall GPA

> Bold type and varied font size add emphasis.

Related Coursework:

Hotel/Resort Management and Development	Resort Programming
Tourism and Travel	Computer Applications
Budgeting and Finance	Resort Marketing
Labor Relations	International Business

Special Project: Student Tour Representative. Conducted feasibility analysis for Overseas Adventures European Travel Company. Helped to organize advertising, marketing, and selling of tour to potential clients (DATES).

Awards

- Selected as member of Outstanding College Students of America (DATE)
- Five-time Dean's Honor List Student
- Awarded Certificate with Honors from American Hotel and Motel Association by successfully completing Resort Management course with an overall score of 90% or better
- Recipient of $1,000 Rollins Merit Award from Minnesota State (DATE)
- Recipient of $4,000 Hillsborough Village Scholarship (DATE)

Experience

Recreation Center Program Assistant. Blair House: Minnesota State University at Manaugua, MN Recruited, selected, and trained Recreation Attendants. Supervised day-to-day activities of nine attendants and seven aerobic instructors. Responsible for collecting aerobic fees and managing center budget. Used a computer to produce monthly newsletter and provided advertising for all activities. Organized athletic tournaments and leagues. Served as co-advisor of on-campus Activities Planning Team (DATES).

> Include internships and other course-related experiences.

Summer Conference Assistant. Student Life: Minnesota State University at Manaugua, MN Supervised and assigned desk hours to Front Desk Clerks. Organized staff payroll records. Organized and secured facilities as requested by conference groups. Met with conference group leaders and operated as primary contact person for assigned groups. Coordinated meal plans and billing services for conference groups with University Food Service. Assisted and coordinated the check-in and check-out process for groups. Responsible on an "on call" basis. Enforced university policies and confronted violators (DATES).

Student Intern. Fairfield Lodge and Resort: Fairfield Springs, MN Implemented planned programs and supervised group activities and special events. Trained in retail sales, bookkeeping and depositing, marketing, safety and liability, and recreation programming (DATES).

Activities

Member of Student Commercial Recreation Association
Member of Minnesota Parks and Recreation Association
Vice President, MSU Business Club

> Optional

Interests

Outdoor recreation, physical fitness, and international relations

SAMPLE PRINT RÉSUMÉ #2

TAMMY S. WILSON

PERMANENT ADDRESS   **LOCAL ADDRESS**
4203 West Erie   8607 Wesley
Erie, PA 16000   600 East Pennsylvania
(814) 000-0000   Longley, PA 16703
                                                                                   (814) 000-0000

EDUCATION   **Bachelor of Science in Recreation and Parks**
                     Erie State University, Erie, PA
                     Anticipated Graduation: (DATE)
                     Emphasis Area: Therapeutic Recreation
                     Minor: Psychology
                     Overall GPA: 3.93/4.00

OTHER   *Therapeutic Recreation Research and Evaluation: A Seminar for Practitioners*
EDUCATIONAL   at the Erie State Hospital, Erie, PA
EXPERIENCES   *Therapeutic Recreation and Community Re-Entry Programs for Persons with
                     Head Injuries* presentation by Dr. Joanne Alexander from East Coast Reha-
                     bilitation Centers, Philadelphia, PA

PROFESSIONAL EXPERIENCE

> Specify volunteer and part-time positions.

Children's Rehabilitation Home, Beach City, NJ   (DATES)

Position: Independent Study Student (Volunteer)
Responsibilities: Supervised, encouraged, and ensured the safety of patients participating in recreational activities. Documented patient participation as well as incidents witnessed. Also assisted with community outings that involved transferring patients, loading/unloading equipment, driving hospital vehicles, and professionally representing the hospital to the public while protecting individual patients' rights to privacy. In addition, planned and conducted one-on-one sessions with a child with a traumatic brain injury, assisted with special physical therapy/therapeutic recreation programs, and helped orient and supervise volunteers.

Position: Receptionist (Part-time)
Responsibilities: Coordinated communication between outside callers and hospital staff by receiving and transmitting calls (including paging hospital personnel) to proper destinations within the hospital. Also provided information and passes for visitors, contacted emergency services when necessary, and professionally represented the hospital to the public.

Position: "Thumper" (Part-time)
Responsibilities: Performed postural drainage on children with cystic fibrosis. Also documented condition of the child and the characteristics of the expelled mucus.

Office of Disability Services, Erie State, Erie, PA   (DATES)

Position: Proctor (Part-time)
Responsibilities: Assisted students with disabilities in taking exams (including returning completed exams to instructors).

College Settlement Program, Hollidaysville, PA   (DATES)

Position: Environmentalist
Responsibilities: Programmed and conducted environmental activities (including spelunking) for inner-city children ages seven through twelve. Also supervised counselors during small group activities.

SAMPLE PRINT RÉSUMÉ #2 (continued)

T. WILSON   Page 2

OTHER EXPERIENCE

Audio Visual Services, Erie State, Erie, PA   (DATE) - Present

Position: Projectionist (Part-time)
Responsibilities: Cooperating with faculty members to provide audiovisual services for university classes.

Cashew World II, Atlantic City, NJ   (DATES)

Position: Cashier (Part-time)
Responsibilities: Handled daily receipts and provided information for tourists.

Student Recruitment Task Force, East Comus, PA   (DATES)

Position: Student Recruiter (Volunteer)
Responsibilities: Planned and conducted presentation designed to recruit high school students for the Erie State University.

COMPUTER EXPERIENCE	Knowledge of both IBM and Macintosh computers Familiar with Word Perfect, Microsoft Word, Quicken, Adobe Photoshop, FileMaker Pro, and other software programs.
CURRENT CERTIFICATIONS	Advanced First Aid, expires (DATE) Cardiopulmonary Resuscitation, expires (DATE)

Include expiration dates for certifications.

PROFESSIONAL INVOLVEMENT	Helping Hand Program, (DATES) **Assistant Director**, (DATE) - Present. Erie State University Recreation and Parks Society, (DATE) - Present. **Secretary**, (DATES) Center for Counseling and Psychological Services Advisory Board, (DATE) - Present. **Cofounder.** Interest Group Related to Persons with Disabilities, (DATES) **Cofounder.**

Joining organizations demonstrates professional commitment.

HONORS	Recreation and Parks (YEAR) Services Junior Merit Scholarship Award College of Health and Human Development Academic Achievement Scholarship Golden Key National Honor Society Outstanding College Students of America University Scholar's Program, (DATES) Dean's List, Fall (YEAR) through Spring (YEAR)
INTERESTS	Ice skating, rappelling, hiking, caving, fishing, canoeing, reading, aerobics.

Optional

SAMPLE PRINT RÉSUMÉ #3

KELLY S. CRAIG

Permanent Address	**Present Address**
1 Court Street	40 West 2nd Avenue, 19F
Mile High, CO 80621	Thorton, CO 80703
(000) 267-4000	(000) 894-1296

> Use of lines may improve balance and appearance.

EDUCATION

Mountain State University at Rockies, Rockies, Colorado
Bachelor of Arts, Business Management: Expected (DATE)
Concentration: International Business and Finance

PROFESSIONAL EXPERIENCE

Vice-President. Associated Students, Inc., Mountain State University at Rockies (DATES). Elected by student body to position of Chief Operating Officer of $14 million, 16,000 member corporation that operates campus bookstore, food services, student government, and student union with a staff of 500 employees. Promoted and facilitated open communication throughout the corporation by effective verbal and written directives and memorandums. Conducted staff assessments. Aided implementation of reorganized managerial structure. Successfully lobbied bill that obtained temporary injunction after a takeover attempt. Additional accomplishments:

> Bulleted statements can emphasize accomplishments.

- Coordinated extensive recruitment drive that placed 200 students on government boards.

- Designed new officer orientation and training program.

- Programmed and budgeted two three-day retreats with a $3,000 budget. Coordinated divergent groups including businesses, management, and service components.

- Organized and conducted campus-wide student leadership seminar for 2,000 faculty, staff, and students. Topics included stress management, fund raising, educational equity, and effective meeting techniques.

Recreation Leader. Western Parks and Recreation Department, Johnson, Colorado (DATES). Planned and supervised daily activities for youth ages 6 to 16. Designed promotional material including flyers, posters, and release forms. Worked effectively with participants, as well as public and private agency officials.

Wellness Consultant. Lifestyle Wellness Systems, Mountain State University at Rockies (DATES). Instructed weekly wellness programs for university students and management level employees for community-based commercial organizations. Instructed in areas of time management, stress management, visualization, and goal setting.

SAMPLE PRINT RÉSUMÉ #3 (continued)

KELLY S. CRAIG
Page 2

PROFESSIONAL EXPERIENCE
(continued)

Recreation Leader. Mile High YMCA, Mile High, Colorado (DATES). Led overnight and extended stay camps for youth ages 10 to 18. Responsible for special events at extended stay camps including Farewell Dinner, Counselor Comedy Night, and Fireside Skit Night.

Waitress, Hostess, Cashier. The Noodle House (DATES); Two Guys From Greece, Mile High, Colorado (DATES). Greeted customers, received and placed orders, delivered meals, worked directly with the public, coworkers, and management. Responded to a variety of requests quickly, efficiently, and accurately under pressure.

> Computer skills may enhance your value to an agency.

COMPUTER SKILLS

Experienced with IBM computers using Windows format and a variety of software packages including Microsoft Word, PageMaker, Microsoft Excel, and QuickBooks.

AFFILIATIONS

Vice-President Coordinator, Recreation Students Association (DATES)

Founder, Vice-President, Social Director, Generating Developmental Ideas (GDI) (DATES). Created the largest service and social organization on university's campus.

Women's Council of the Mountain State University (DATES)

Pledge Class President, Service Chairperson, Alpha Chi Alpha National Sorority (DATES)

RELATED ACTIVITIES

President, on-campus residence hall (DATES)
President, Inter-hall President's Council (DATES)
Varsity Diving Team (DATES)
Freshman Orientation Leader (DATES)
Student Academic Affairs Council (DATES)
Student Organization and Activities Council (DATES)
Student Advisory Committee (DATES)

REFERENCES

Father Terrance McCann
St. Mary's Church
1400 York Road
Middletown, CO 80591
(000) 647-2000

Dr. Jerome Farthinger
Associate Professor
Mountain State University
Rockies, CO 80700
(000) 742-0000

Mary S. Ludwig
14 Westerly Parkway
Middletown, CO 80591
(000) 901-9000

William Morris
Program Director
Western Parks and Recreation Department
Johnson, CO 80412
(000) 640-0000

SAMPLE PRINT RÉSUMÉ #4

Christy Lewis

1100 Hobart Street
Razorback, Arkansas 72601
(501) 342-1000

Education
Mississippi Valley University, Razorback, Arkansas
Bachelor of Arts, Psychology and Therapeutic Recreation: Anticipated (DATE)

Related Coursework:

Leisure Counseling	Abnormal Psychology
Therapeutic Recreation Techniques	Counseling Psychology
Therapeutic Recreation Services	Drug Use and Abuse
Programming for Special Populations	Early Childhood Development

Corle College: Corle, California
Associate of Arts, Psychology: (DATE)

> Listing related courses can emphasize areas of expertise.

Experience
SMITH DEVELOPMENTAL CENTER, "CAMP VIA": Elderidge, Arkansas
Camp Counselor. Created and implemented daily recreation programs as part of treatment team. Supervised and aided clients in activities of daily living and encouraged socialization (DATES).

COMMUNITY LIVING CENTER, RIVERSIDE: Paradise, Arkansas
House Counselor. Implemented individualized program plans and supervised clients in daily life skills. Recorded each client's activities and daily programs. Supervised evening recreation group and community interaction group. Assisted clients with conflict resolution. Maintained chart points for day and administered medication. Prepared balanced meals for residents and shopped for groceries. Transported clients to medical appointments and recreation activities (DATES).

Programmer. Implemented individualized program plans and supervised clients in daily life skills. Led evening recreation group and community interaction group. Served as advocate for clients. Maintained client behavior records (DATES).

JACK'S RESTAURANT: Lempert, Mississippi
Waitress. Evening Dining Room. Performed customer service. Took orders, added tickets, and served food (DATES).

SAINT THOMAS MEDICAL CENTER: Burton, Arkansas
Secretary/Radiology. Answered phones and transferred calls to appropriate source. Typed forms, memos, and various reports. Accepted deliveries (DATES).

CAMP ABILITY: Westonville, Arkansas
Counselor Aide. Supervised eight campers with developmental disabilities, 6 to 8 years old. Organized group activities. Assisted with behavior management (DATES).

SAMPLE PRINT RÉSUMÉ #4 (continued)

Christy Lewis
Page 2

Volunteer Experience	SMITH DEVELOPMENTAL CENTER: Elderidge, Arkansas Organized Community Action Volunteers in Education (CAVE) weekend workshop. Counseled clients with severe developmental disabilities on behavior unit (DATES). MEG TAYLOR'S ADULT DAY PROGRAM: Pendleton, Arkansas Taught dancing skills to older adults in adaptive dance program (DATES). SOCIAL ADVOCATES FOR YOUTH (S.A.Y.): Westbrook, Arkansas Worked at facility for adolescents with mental illness, including physically and sexually abused youth. Responsible for implementation of behavior modification program and enforcement of house policies and procedures. Reviewed individual program plans and histories. Assisted in case staff meetings with senior S.A.Y. staff (DATES). DEAL DEVELOPMENTAL CENTER: Westbrook, Arkansas Assisted children with developmental disabilities (6 to 12 years old) with leisure activities. Worked under the supervision of certified recreational therapist and consultant for North American Health Care Unlimited (DATES). LAMPLOC DAY TREATMENT CENTER: Westbrook, Arkansas. Led recreational activities for youth and adults with mental illnesses. Supervised clients in meal preparation, ceramics, and sports activities. Participated in Group Therapy sessions led by licensed clinical psychologist (DATES).
Special Skills and Activities	• Certificate in Wilderness Leadership, Mississippi Valley University • Cardiopulmonary Resuscitation (CPR). Expires (DATE) • Advanced First Aid. Expires (DATE) • Member, Arkansas Park and Recreation Society (APRS) • Water Safety Instructor (WSI). Expires (DATE) **Interests:** Aerobics, backpacking, cross-country skiing, travel (backpacked through Europe), nutrition, outdoor adventure for persons with disabilities.

References should be included on résumé or attached (see pg. 116).

SAMPLE PRINT RÉSUMÉ #5

Brenda Kathryn Call

729 4th Avenue • San Francisco, CA • 93000 • (000) 893-7777

Education

San Francisco Bay University, San Francisco, CA
Bachelor of Science, Recreation Administration: Date
Option: Community and Commercial Recreation
Minor: Nutrition and Employee Fitness

Related Coursework:

Leadership and Supervision in Recreation	Normal Nutrition
Resort Development and Management	Therapeutic Nutrition
Management of Recreation and Parks	Nutrition and Physical Fitness
Private Enterprise Recreation and Tourism	Nutrition Through Life
Recreation Budget and Finance Management	Body Awareness and Weight Control

Experience

KANGAROO KATIE'S FITNESS CENTER: Ellis, California
Pro Shop/Bookkeeping Assistant. Responsible for scheduling reservations, selling food and beverages, and providing clean, rolled towels, plus a friendly welcome upon each member's entrance. Maintained accurate membership records via data entry, performed budget reconciliation and monthly billing procedures, typed and filed documents (DATES).

SAN FRANCISCO BAY UNIVERSITY, GEOGRAPHY DEPT: San Francisco, California
Secretary. Assisted full-time secretary and worked independently answering and transferring phone calls, typing, photocopying, filing, and performing miscellaneous errands (DATES).

BART'S FITNESS FOR WOMEN: San Francisco, California
Receptionist. Responsible for opening club, selling memberships, and completing contracts, receiving and making phone calls, staffing boutique, and preparing billing. Duties also included Jacuzzi maintenance, bulletin board displays, miscellaneous signs/posters, and some exercise instruction (DATES).

ASSOCIATION FOR RETARDED CITIZENS: Westerly, California
Respite Worker/Day Care Aide. Cared for elderly persons with various disabilities in their homes. Tasks included feeding, bathing, toileting, administering medication, and providing companionship during leisure activities. Also planned and programmed after school activities for ages 4 to 10 elementary-school children three days per week (DATES).

RECREATION HOUSE FOR THE HANDICAPPED: Ellis, California
Program Leader Substitute. Assisted in programming and implementing numerous activities mainly in adult day care departments. Duties included supervision of volunteers and implementation of behavior modification techniques (DATES).

JODY AND ASSOCIATES: Ellis, California
Respite Worker. Provided in-home care for children with disabilities and completed activity reports following every assignment (DATES).

SAMPLE PRINT RÉSUMÉ #5 (continued)

Brenda Kathryn Call *Page 2*

Experience (Cont'd)

PLEASANTVILLE PARKS AND RECREATION DISTRICT: Pleasantville, California
Gymnastics Coach. Enabled 5 to 15 year old girls to improve abilities in gymnastics. Coordinated presentations of their talents following each four-week session (DATES).

DORSHALL'S INC.: Titus, California
Cashier. Operated cash register for retail clothing chain; named fastest cashier in district. Trained and supervised new employees (DATES).

Other Information

- Merit Internship Program
- Student Dietetic Association
- Cardiopulmonary Resuscitation (CPR)
- American Sign Language Course
- Competed in the Pan American Games (Gymnastics), Puerto Rico
- Travel experience in Spain, France, U.S. Virgin Islands, Hawaii, and Mexico.

Interests

Nutrition and wellness, aerobics, biking, weight training, gymnastics, camping, and waterskiing.

> Listing interests can demonstrate possession of job-related skills.

References

> References can be used to complete a two-page résumé.

Thomas E. Johnson, Ph.D.
Department of Recreation and Parks Management
San Francisco Bay University
San Francisco, California 94100
(415) 898-6000

Katie Wells
Manager, Kangaroo Katie's Fitness Center
1026 Skyline Drive
Ellis, California 92001
(415) 895-6000

Scott Azinger
12 N. 8th Street, S.W.
Spokane, Washington 96000
(509) 527-7000

Johnny Pensic
Network System Manager, Instructional Media Center
San Francisco Bay University
San Francisco, California 94100
(415) 895-2000

SAMPLE PRINT RÉSUMÉ #6

Beth Wells

555 W. 12th Street. Sacramento, CA 95816   916-451-3333   916-451-1111(cell)   bwells66@aol.com

Available: September 2007, willing to relocate anywhere.

PROFILE Highly motivated, independent woman seeking a full-time position in the hospitality industry. Well-traveled and independent, in reference to new experiences and geographical locations. Familiarity with Spanish and French and has lived and worked in Spain. Computer literate and trained in many software programs. Born leader and willing to lead by example for others. Exceeds expectations, detailed-oriented, and has strong skills in multi-tasking. Excellent presentational and communication skills, both orally and written.

EDUCATION

CALIFORNIA STATE UNIVERSITY, SACRAMENTO
Bachelor of Science: Hospitality Management
Minor: Business Management
Earned 90% of all college expenses

Related Coursework:

Hotel Management	Budget & Finance
Hotel Operations	Business Accounting
Customer Service & Sales	Business Law
Marketing	Business Communications

Barcelona Management Institute, Spain
International Business & Hospitality Administration

EXPERIENCE

Management Experience. Roseville, CA
Assistant Manager, Gourmet Food, Inc.   (DATES)
- Demonstrate excellent food knowledge within the gourmet food industry
- Management tasks: Payroll, Scheduling, Opening/Closing, Hiring & Training
- Provided excellent customer service and displayed merchandise

Resident Hall, CSU, Sacramento
Resident Advisor   (DATES)
- Advised 35 first-year female students
- Worked with a staff of 2 Resident Advisors to provide support and encouragement
- Enforced policy to uphold University vision and goals
- Provided and built an approachable atmosphere where students would feel safe

Belmont Towers Bed & Breakfast Inn
Assistant Office Manager   (DATES)
- Checked guests in/out
- Provided outstanding customer service
- Prepared occupancy information
- Employee of the month twice

SAMPLE PRINT RÉSUMÉ #7

MILES DAVIS

mdavis76lb@hotmail.com

333 Hope Drive
Blacksburg, VA 24061

540-231-0000 (cell)

OBJECTIVE

To obtain an internship in community recreation that will further develop my skills in communication, programming, community development, diversity, problem solving, and leadership.

STRENGTHS

- Ability to work in a team environment and support other members
- Self-motivated with high energy and enthusiasm
- Strong leadership and motivational skills
- Extensive background in programming and fundraising
- Knowledge of a wide range of computer programs: Excel, PowerPoint, Camtasia, Web 2.0

EDUCATION

Virginia Tech, Blacksburg, VA
Master's: Recreation Administration
Option: Community/Commercial Recreation
West Virginia State University, WV
Bachelor's: Recreation Management
Option: Nonprofits and Fundraising

EXPERIENCE

Recreation Supervisor, Blacksburg Recreation & Parks Department
- Directly supervised 5 recreation and 15 after school specialists
- Designed and implemented programming models
- Delegated jobs and responsibilities to appropriate staff
- Served as team trainer and leader

Resident Advisor, West Virginia State
- Supervised coed residence hall floor community (80 students)
- Monitored and enforced University policies
- Assumed staff leadership position and training of new advisors
- Served on staff council
- Coordinated activities and programs regarding first-year students
- Trained in emergency procedures and stress management

Recreation Intramurals Coordinator, Penn State
- Created and programmed college-wide intramural programs
- Worked as a team member of 15 coordinators
- Prepared public relations brochures, budgets, and program evaluations

HONORS

Virginia Tech, Computer Lab Assistant
Residence Hall Advisor of the Year
Dean's list all four semesters at West Virginia State
President, West Virginia State Recreation Club

SAMPLE PRINT REFERENCE LIST

MILES DAVIS

REFERENCES

Dr. Wendell Carson
Professor
Department of Recreation Administration
West Virginia State University
Lexington, WV 30002
Phone: (000) 555-8374
Fax: (000) 555-8232
E-mail: wpearson@wvsu.edu

Rev. Cheryl P. Makover
Pastor
Congregational Methodist Church
999 Westmoreland Drive
Mortonville, WV 30000
Phone: (000) 651-8989
Fax: (000) 651-0000
E-mail: prayer@access.com

Perry Pennypacker
Director of Marketing
Lifestyle Associates
RR #2
Lexington, WV 30005
Phone: (000) 555-6666
Fax: (000) 555-6667

Paige Gribaldi
19 Jacob's Way
Mortonville, WV 30000
Phone: (000) 733-8765

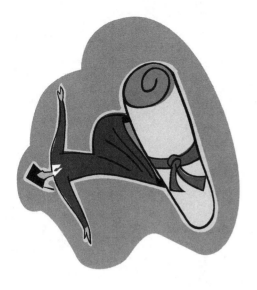

WILLIAM ANDERSON
222 NORD AVENUE
Chico, CA 95926

530-899-8000

530-518-4422 (cell)

Available after June 21, 2013

www.wanderson21yahoo.com

COVER LETTER

During my college career, I have worked in a variety of settings. In those experiences, I have been fascinated with program development and implementation. These experiences have helped me to focus on my career goals and objectives of providing quality recreational services.

Academically, I am in the top fifteen percent of my class, and in the top five percent of the Recreation majors. I am dedicated to the Recreation field and have proved this by my extensive work experience and involvement with the Recreation Club, an affiliation of the National Recreation & Park Association. I am also a member of the California Recreation & Park Society and the California Special Events Association.

I am looking for a semester-long internship that would provide me with the challenges and knowledge of a mid-level recreation supervisor within a community setting. Your agency would be a perfect environment for me to learn and grow professionally. This to me is not only an internship, but a career move as well.

Please review the resume on the inner-portion and my business work experiences. Thank you for your time!

Sincerely,

William Anderson

POSITION DESIRED

Seeking an internship with challenges, rewards, and the ability to use my organizational skills and attention to detail while helping to further the skills of others.

EDUCATION

California State University, Chico

BS: Recreation Administration DATE

Options: Community Recreation

Special Events Management

Fluent in Spanish and conversational Italian

Computer Skills: Microsoft Word, Excel, PowerPoint, QuickTime, Publisher, Outlook, Adobe Photoshop

Dean's List all four years

President/Social Chair, Recreation Majors Club

Related Courses:

- Leadership/Supervision
- Budget & Finance
- Marketing/Promotions
- Business Law
- Business Correspondence
- Programming
- Customer Service/Sales
- Special Events Management
- Human Resources

BUSINESS EXPERIENCE

Convention Services Assistant

- Assist Convention Services Manager
- Prepare financial reports
- Supervise special events
- Train staff
- Schedule staff
- Prepare event proposals
- Awarded employee of the year

Intramural Coordinator

- Supervised campus-wide sports programs.
- Worked as part of a team of 6 coordinators
- Fundraising skills
- Brochure/flyer development
- Trained intramural assistants

AFTER SCHOOL ASSISTANT

- Assisted in the coordination of 3 programs.
- Developed and created recreation and education programs for elementary school students.
- Supported teachers goals for each student involved in the program

BUSINESS AND PERSONAL SKILLS

- Strong interpersonal and communication skills (written and oral)
- Resourceful and self-confident
- Remain calm and work well under demanding conditions
- Proven leadership and supervision skills
- Enjoy creating and preparing programs
- Understand budgets and financial statements
- Highly effective in promoting a positive and productive work environment
- Work independently and as part of a team
- Ability to prioritize, delegate and motivate
- Able to accept challenges and problem-solving
- Quick learner and ability to adapt
- Ability to meet deadlines and work with minimal supervision

Lead white water guide

JOHN BOOTH
123 8TH AVENUE
Chico, CA 95926

530-345-0070

530-518-1212 (cell)

johnclass5@yahoo.com

TRIPS LED BY JOHN BOOTH

Trip to Vancouver, Canada

Camping in desert

Climbing in Utah

COVER LETTER

I was put in contact with you through Jake Myers at CSU, Chico Adventure Outings. I was made aware of your Outdoor Adventure Specialist internship and I enclose my resume in application for this role.

My experience as an outdoors person has included a three-year position as rafting supervisor and guide where I had direct responsibility for outdoor trips and 25+ employees. Prior to that I was a senior trip leader for the City of Carlsbad, CA, where I supervised employees and managed all aspects of ocean activities.

With my successful management experience and proven track record in outdoor and wilderness adventures, I feel that I would be a valuable addition to your company. I enclose my résumé for your attention and hope that if you have any questions that require clarification you will not hesitate to contact me at the above telephone numbers.

I would like to meet with you personally to discuss this further and will contact you within the next week to arrange a meeting that is convenient for you.

Sincerely,

John Booth

POSITION DESIRED

Seeking an internship working as a team leader with challenging adventures. Able to use the skills and knowledge learning in college.

EDUCATION

California State University, Chico

BS: Recreation Administration DATE

Options: Community Recreation

Natural Resource

Management

Fluent in Spanish

Computer Skills: Microsoft Word, Excel, PowerPoint, QuickTime, Publisher, Outlook, Adobe Photoshop

3.5 GPA

Related Courses:

- Leadership/Management
- Budget & Finance
- Marketing/Promotions
- Business Law
- Business Ethics
- Programming
- Natural Resource Management
- Natural Resource Development
- Environmental Education

BUSINESS EXPERIENCE

OUTDOOR ADVENTURE SUPERVISOR & GUIDE

- Assistant business manager
- Prepared schedules
- Responsible for training guides
- First aid preparedness
- Equipment inventory
- Oversee trips
- Worked on legal aspects

SENIOR TRIP LEADER

- Lead outdoor adventure outings
- Public speaking
- Managing people and equipment
- Trip planning and logistics
- Following policies and procedures

HEAD LIFEGUARD

- Oversee swimming facilities
- Conducted lifeguard training and CPR
- Conducted swim lesson classes
- Responsible for scheduling

BUSINESS AND PERSONAL SKILLS

- Strong interpersonal and communication skills (written and oral)
- Resourceful and self-confident
- Remain calm and work well under demanding conditions
- Proven leadership and supervision skills
- Enjoy creating and preparing programs
- Understand budgets and financial statements
- Highly effective in promoting a positive and productive work environment
- Work independently and as part of a team
- Ability to prioritize, delegate and motivate
- Able to accept challenges and problem-solving
- Quick learner and ability to adapt
- Ability to meet deadlines and work with minimal supervision

Exercise Time

Now that you have seen some good examples of print résumés, let's look at two that contain errors and omissions. Exercises 5.2 and 5.3 provide practice in identifying errors and omissions in print résumés. These exercises are identical to the cover letter exercises you completed in Chapter Four. At this point, test your understanding of résumés by circling the errors and missing information. Then check your answers against the errors and omissions we identified.

Exercise 5.2: Résumé Corrections Exercise

Deborah Susan Jeffcoat
750 University Drive
Staunton, CT 06900

INTERNSHIP OBJECTIVE

To obtain an internship in the field of Parks and Recreation with an emphasis on Visitor Management and Law Enforcement.

EDUCATION

Bachelor of Science: Recreation and Parks
Option: Outdoor Recreation
New England University
University City, CT 06913

ACTIVITIES

Student Conservation Club (DATES)
New England University Outing Club (DATES)
Secretary (DATES)
Connecticut Recreation and Parks Association—Student Branch (DATES)

WORK EXPERIENCE

(DATE) to Present   Connecticut State Parks
PATROLMAN II   Hilltop Pond State Park
                                     Jacobyville, CT

Responsible for providing public safety through law enforcement action and visitor information. Duties included: Patroling park, campground, beaches, and nearby boat landings and waterways; keeping daily logs and records, assisting public with information, first aid, and emergency situations; and maintaining equipment and facilities. Successfully completed Connecticut State Parks law enforcement training.

(DATES)   Blueberry Fields, Inc.
RESIDENTIAL COUNSELOR   West Chester, VT

Responsible for instruction and supervision of children and adults with mental disabilities. Duties included: Assisting in daily living skills; counseling clients in areas of personal development, socialization, and coping skills; maintaining daily logs; and participating in staff meetings, etc.

(DATES)   City of Hillsdale
TRAIL SUPERVISOR   Goode Environmental Area
(Volunteer)   Hillsdale, VT

Responsible for trail maintenance. Duties included: Supervision of teenage volunteer staff; conducting periodic inspections of designated trails; and maintaining records on designated trails.

Page 2

WORK EXPERIENCE	(DATES) **CLERK** (Part-time)	Curriculum Materials Center New England University University City, CT

Responsible for front desk operations. Duties included: Providing information; arranging and locating reserve materials; assisting students; and shelving resources. Also assisted in typing, labeling, and designing display cases.

	(DATES) **FOREST SERVICE VOLUNTEER**	USDA Forest Service Manstone National Forest

Duties included patrolling campsites and river landings, providing visitor information and ensuring good public relations, and maintaining trails. Also assisted in law enforcement, front desk, office duties, and map work. Conducted tours for school-age children. Qualified as National Forest Firefighter.

	(DATES) **CANVASSER**	Public Interest Coalition Inquiry, CT

Duties included: Presenting information on important economic and political issues to the public; requesting donations; and training new employees. Also attended relevant workshops and training sessions.

CERTIFICATIONS	Advanced First Aid and Emergency Care Cardiopulmonary Resuscitation (CPR) Red Card—National Forest Firefighter

PERSONAL DATA	Height:	5' 6"
	Weight:	125 lbs.
	Marital Status:	Single
	Health:	Excellent

REFERENCES	Penny Martin Bethlehem Industries 478 Industry Drive University City, CT 06913	James A. Baldwin Assistant Professor New England University University City, CT 06913

Answers to 5.2

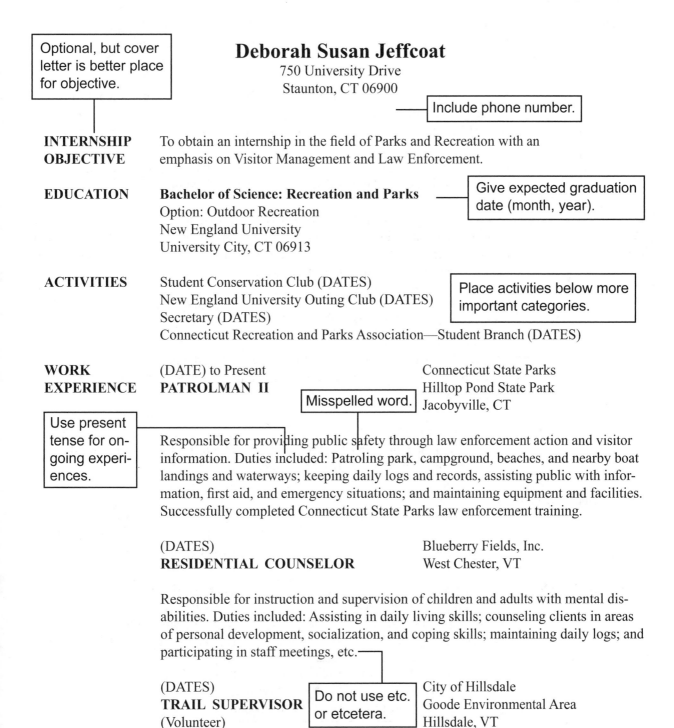

Optional, but cover letter is better place for objective.

Deborah Susan Jeffcoat
750 University Drive
Staunton, CT 06900

Include phone number.

INTERNSHIP OBJECTIVE   To obtain an internship in the field of Parks and Recreation with an emphasis on Visitor Management and Law Enforcement.

EDUCATION   **Bachelor of Science: Recreation and Parks**
Option: Outdoor Recreation
New England University
University City, CT 06913

Give expected graduation date (month, year).

ACTIVITIES   Student Conservation Club (DATES)
New England University Outing Club (DATES)
Secretary (DATES)
Connecticut Recreation and Parks Association—Student Branch (DATES)

Place activities below more important categories.

WORK EXPERIENCE   (DATE) to Present   Connecticut State Parks
PATROLMAN II   Hilltop Pond State Park
                                           Jacobyville, CT

Misspelled word.

Use present tense for on-going experiences.

Responsible for providing public safety through law enforcement action and visitor information. Duties included: Patroling park, campground, beaches, and nearby boat landings and waterways; keeping daily logs and records, assisting public with information, first aid, and emergency situations; and maintaining equipment and facilities. Successfully completed Connecticut State Parks law enforcement training.

(DATES)   Blueberry Fields, Inc.
RESIDENTIAL COUNSELOR   West Chester, VT

Responsible for instruction and supervision of children and adults with mental disabilities. Duties included: Assisting in daily living skills; counseling clients in areas of personal development, socialization, and coping skills; maintaining daily logs; and participating in staff meetings, etc.

Do not use etc. or etcetera.

(DATES)   City of Hillsdale
TRAIL SUPERVISOR   Goode Environmental Area
(Volunteer)   Hillsdale, VT

Responsible for trail maintenance. Duties included: Supervision of teenage volunteer staff; conducting periodic inspections of designated trails; and maintaining records on designated trails.

Be sure name is at top
of second page.

Page 2

WORK   (DATES)   Curriculum Materials Center
EXPERIENCE   **CLERK** (Part-time)   New England University
                                                     University City, CT

Indicate category
is continued from
previous page.

    Responsible for front desk operations. Duties included: Providing information; arranging and locating reserve materials; assisting students; and shelving resources. Also assisted in typing, labeling, and designing display cases.

Need city
and state.

    (DATES)   USDA Forest Service
FOREST SERVICE VOLUNTEER   Manstone National Forest

Be consistent;
not indented on
the first page.

    Duties included patrolling campsites and river landings, providing visitor information and ensuring good public relations, and maintaining trails. Also assisted in law enforcement, front desk, office duties, and map work. Conducted tours for school-age children. Qualified as National Forest Firefighter.

    (DATES)   Public Interest Coalition
CANVASSER   Inquiry, CT

Be consistent;
use colon here.

    Duties included: Presenting information on important economic and political issues to the public; requesting donations; and training new employees. Also attended relevant workshops and training sessions.

CERTIFICATIONS   Advanced First Aid and Emergency Care
                        Cardiopulmonary Resuscitation (CPR)
                        Red Card—National Forest Firefighter

Include expiration dates.

PERSONAL DATA   Height: 5' 6"
                        Weight: 125 lbs.
                        Marital Status: Single
                        Health: Excellent

Do not include
personal data.

REFERENCES   Penny Martin   James A. Baldwin
                        Bethlehem Industries   Assistant Professor
                        478 Industry Drive   New England University
                        University City, CT 06913   University City, CT 06913

Need Penny's title, Penny's and
James' phone numbers, and a
total of three or four references.

Exercise 5.3: Résumé Corrections Exercise

WILLIAM PEPPER

2000 North Hollen Way   San Jose, CA 94128   (408) 722-1200

EDUCATION

Leland Surfer University
B.S. Degree: (DATE)
Minor: Gerontology
Anticipated Graduation: (DATE)

Related Coursework:

Anatomy	Programming for Special Populations
Physiology	Leisure Counseling
Social Gerontology	Therapeutic Recreation Services
College Algebra	Therapeutic Recreation Techniques
Aging and Leisure	Therapeutic Case Management

EXPERIENCE

Sierra Home and Village, San Diego, CA   (DATES)
Therapeutic Recreation Director: Responsible for providing therapeutic recreation and social programming for complex of 200 adult residents. Duties: I assess needs, develop and implement programs, meet with medical staff, attend team meetings, and provide community awareness. Also supervise staff of 3 TR assistants and trained volunteers.

Lynbrook Community Center, Lynbrook, CA   (DATES)
Recreation Coordinator: Responsible for program development and implementation for older adults in a community setting. Duties: I scheduled activities and entertainment, provided community awareness training, coordinated community outings, and trained volunteers.

Hartswick Veterans Home, Hartswick, CA   (DATES)
Recreation Supervisor: Responsible for therapeutic recreation programming for residents within medical treatment program. Duties: I conducted assessments through interviews and observations, charted progress of residents, evaluated effectiveness of programs, initiated appropriate referrals, and participated in interdisciplinary team meetings. I also supervised staff of 5 technicians and trained volunteers.

Broughton City Parks and Recreation, Broughton, CA   (DATES)
Recreation Leader: Responsible for providing community recreation for people with special needs. Duties: Special events, community trips, leisure awareness classes, and socialization training.

CERTIFICATIONS

Multi-Media Standard First Aid (Expiration: DATE)
Therapeutic Recreation Specialist, California Board of Park and Recreation Personnel

Answers to 5.3

WILLIAM PEPPER

2000 North Hollen Way   San Jose, CA 94128   (408) 722-1200

EDUCATION

Leland Surfer University
B.S. Degree: (DATE)
Minor: Gerontology
Anticipated Graduation: (DATE)

> Include city and state of university plus major.

Related Coursework:

Anatomy	Programming for Special Populations
Physiology	Leisure Counseling
Social Gerontology	Therapeutic Recreation Services
College Algebra	Therapeutic Recreation Techniques
Aging and Leisure	Therapeutic Case Management

> Include only courses related to major/option.

EXPERIENCE

Sierra Home and Village, San Diego, CA   (DATES)
Therapeutic Recreation Director: Responsible for providing therapeutic recreation and social programming for complex of 200 adult residents. Duties: I assess needs, develop and implement programs, meet with medical staff, attend team meetings, and provide community awareness. Also supervise staff of 3 TR assistants and trained volunteers.

Lynbrook Community Center, Lynbrook, CA   (DATES)
Recreation Coordinator: Responsible for program development and implementation for older adults in a community setting. Duties: I scheduled activities and entertainment, provided community awareness training, coordinated community outings, and trained volunteers.

Hartswick Veterans Home, Hartswick, CA   (DATES)
Recreation Supervisor: Responsible for therapeutic recreation programming for residents within medical treatment program. Duties: I conducted assessments through interviews and observations, charted progress of residents, evaluated effectiveness of programs, initiated appropriate referrals, and participated in interdisciplinary team meetings. I also supervised staff of 5 technicians and trained volunteers.

> Do not use personal pronouns.

Broughton City Parks and Recreation, Broughton, CA   Summers 1987, 1988
Recreation Leader: Responsible for providing community recreation for people with special needs. Duties: Special events, community trips, leisure awareness classes, and socialization training.

> Need action verb here.

CERTIFICATIONS

Multi-Media Standard First Aid (Expiration: DATE)
Therapeutic Recreation Specialist, California Board of Park and Recreation Personnel

> Be consistent with typefaces.

Scannable Résumés

Many agencies are using scannable résumés to electronically search through résumés for qualified candidates. Typically, a résumé is scanned by a computer using the latest document imaging Optical Character Recognition (OCR) technology. This enables organizations to store résumés and search résumé databases for potential employees. A scannable résumé can be viewed by a computer using the latest document imaging technology, allowing employers to store résumés in databases and search through many applicants electronically using keywords. Generally, the content scannable résumé parallels the content of a traditional print résumé, but there are a couple of notable differences.

Keywords

One major difference is that electronic and scannable résumés should emphasize profession-related nouns, rather than "action verbs." This is important because electronic and scannable résumés are scanned, using keyword or key phrase searches, to select applicants who have specific skills that the employer is seeking. If these skills (i.e., keywords, key phrases) do not appear on your electronic or scannable résumé, you will not be selected for further consideration.

Just below your name on your résumé, you can create a Keyword section (similar to other categories in your résumé: Education, Professional Experience, Skills, etc.). List professionally applicable words and phrases potential employers can search for in the résumé database.

For example, keywords for a therapeutic recreation résumé might include the following:

- Assessment
- Treatment
- Program Planning
- Documentation
- Evaluation
- Disabilities
- Certification

Keywords for a Naturalist might include:

- Leadership
- Program Planning
- Environmental Interpretation
- Instruction
- Resource Management
- Camps
- Special Events

Formatting

Because electronic and scannable résumés are scanned by a computer and not a human, the way information is presented is of paramount importance. It is *essential* to structure the résumé so that it is easily and accurately scanned for content. The following formatting tips will help you prepare your electronic or scannable résumé:

- Save your electronic or scannable résumé as plain text (.txt), Portable Document Format (.pdf), or Rich Text Format (.rtf). This will ensure that your résumé is readable by a wide variety of word processing applications and computer platforms. It also protects against transmitting a virus with your résumé.
- Do not use graphics, lines, shading, boxes, bullets or other such features that might interfere with accurate scanning (dashes are usually effective alternatives to bullets).
- Avoid using italics, bold, or underlines (use upper case to distinguish headings).

- Limit the amount of words, and ensure that there is plenty of white space to avoid errors during scanning.

- Avoid abbreviations, unless universally used and accepted (e.g., state abbreviations such as CA).

- Place telephone area codes within parentheses to ensure recognition by scanners.

- Begin entries on the left margin and avoid unconventional formatting, such as multiple columns. If you choose to indent or center something, it must be done by repeatedly pressing the spacebar. Do not use the tab key or centering option.

- For scannable print résumés, use clear, plain fonts such as Arial, Times, or Helvetica. For size of font, use 11 or 12 points.

- If sending hard copies for scanning, send only originals, mail in a large envelope to avoid folding the résumé, and do not staple two-page résumés.

In summary, using skill-related nouns, including a summary of skills, and adhering to the above formatting tips will ensure an effective electronic or scannable résumé—one that maximizes your chances of being selected for an interview. For more information on scannable résumés, we suggest you visit one of the many career-oriented websites in Appendix A.

Examples of Print Versus Scannable Résumés

The following two résumés are for the same person. The first one (Sample Print Résumé #10) is a traditional print résumé using a variety of effective techniques to emphasize important aspects of the person's academic and work experiences. The second résumé (Sample Scannable Résumé) follows the guidelines for an effective scannable résumé. As you examine these two examples, note the significant differences between a traditional print and scannable résumé.

Required Qualifications

Are there any prerequisites or requirements necessary to qualify for the internship position you want? If certificates (e.g., CPR, Water Safety Instructor) or specific courses are required, make sure you include these qualifications in your cover letter and résumé. If you do not possess the necessary prerequisites or requirements, you need to find out how to obtain these documents or courses. Try to meet all requirements before applying even though some agencies will allow an intern to start the internship while he or she is taking a prerequisite course or certificate program.

Voice Mail/Answering Machine

Voice mail or an answering machine can be a useful tool in your internship search. This allows potential internship supervisors to contact you even while you are away from the phone. Some people do not like answering machines, so make your introductory message brief, positive and, most of all, appropriate. Having a prospective internship supervisor call your voice mail or answering machine when you have a jingle or silly message on it may destroy your chances for the internship you want. Getting a voice mail that answers, "Yo...waz up?" will likely remove you from the agency's list of candidates.

SAMPLE PRINT RÉSUMÉ #10

Terri J. MacDonald
Email: TerriJ@server.net

Permanent Address:	**Present Address:**
8 Stern Avenue	*62A North Shadow Drive*
River View, CA 95309	*Lake View, CA 95310*
(000) 726-1005	*(000) 942-0000*

· **Enthusiastic, energetic, and well-organized.**
· **Ability to prioritize, delegate, and motivate.**
· **Communicate easily with a wide range of personalities.**
· **Able to meet deadlines and work with minimal supervision.**

SKILLS

Computer Experience:
Operating systems: Windows Vista, Windows 7, Windows 8
Applications: Microsoft Office 2010 (Excel, Word, Outlook, and PowerPoint), Sage ACT! 2013 (15.0)
Reservation Systems: MARSHA, PMS, and Richie

Foreign Language:
Four years of Spanish Classes – Spanish 1-3 as well as Conversational Spanish

---

EDUCATION

Brindale University, Lakeland, CA (DATES of attendance)
Bachelor of Science Degree
Major: Recreation Administration: Resort and Lodging Management Option

Relevant Course Work: Merit Internship Program	Communications
Survey of Finance	Foundations of Programming
Recreation Budget/Finance Management	Recreation Employment Law
Commercial Recreation and Tourism	Leisure Services Promotion
Resort and Lodging Operations	Management of Recreation
Leadership and Supervision in Recreation	

College of the West, Glen Ford, CA (DATES of attendance)
Associate in Art Degree in Technical Preparations
Relevant Course Work: Computer Literacy
Accounting

PROFESSIONAL EXPERIENCE

Sales Manager for *"Overnight Inn and Vestibule by Marion–Pleasant Valley"* (DATE of hiring) - Present

Overnight Inn by Marion	Vestibule by Marion
10 Edgewood Drive	Contra Verde Blvd.
Pleasant Valley, CA 94500	Pleasant Valley, CA 94500
(000) 679-8000	(000) 699-2000
Supervisor: Trisha Russell–General Manager	**Supervisor:** Trace More–General Manager

SAMPLE PRINT RÉSUMÉ #10 (continued)

T. MacDonald – Page 2

Manager in Training-Sales at *"Vestibule Inn by Marrion–San Diego"* (DATES of employment)
    12 Win Avenue
    San Diego, CA 92466
    (000) 548-9000
    Supervisor: Niki Deorenzio–Director of Sales
Front Office Intern at *"Palm Springs Rediscovery Resort"* (summer of YEAR)
    22 Sea Side Drive
    Palm Springs, FL 34668
    (000) 324-8888
    Supervisor: Deborah Neal–Front Office Manager
Patient Accounts Clerk at *"Spruce Memorial Hospital"* (summer of YEAR)
    368 Fenner Drive
    North Calvert, CA 99987
    (000) 325-9000
    Supervisor: Dawn J. Lawrence
Customer Service Representative at *"Daisy's Department Store"* (DATES of employment)
    44 Tiaoga Avenue
    Eureka, CA 95503
    (000) 444-9000
    Employer: Merri Bealer
Inn Sitter and Housekeeper at *"Silverster House Bed and Breakfast"* (DATES of employment)
    PO Box 478
    Finney, CA 96445
    (000) 567-6000
    Employers: Ken and Naomi Westland

AWARDS AND ACHIEVEMENTS

Recreation Administration Student of the Year (YEAR)
Soccer Sportsmanship Award (YEAR)

VOLUNTEER WORK

Attended "Marion Student Leadership Summit" (YEARS)
Associated Student Body Vice-President (YEARS)
Toys for Toddlers (YEARS)
Dorothy B. Jackson Center Teen Program (YEARS)

CLUBS/ATHLETICS

Brindale University:
SOLAR (Society of Leisure and Recreation) (YEARS)
President Eta Sigma Chi (Hospitality Management Honor Society) (YEARS)
Community Organization Volunteers in Education (COVE), Big Sister Mentor (YEARS)

SAMPLE ELECTRONIC OR SCANNABLE RÉSUMÉ

Terri J. MacDonald

62A North Shadow Drive
Lake View, CA 95310
(000) 942-0000
Email: TerriJ@server.net

SUMMARY

Study in Recreation Administration, with emphasis in resort and lodging management. Experience in sales and marketing, front office management, accounting, customer service, and housekeeping. Skills include computer competence and conversational Spanish.

COMPUTER SOFTWARE SKILLS

Microsoft Office (Excel, Word, Outlook, PowerPoint), Sage ACT! 2013 (15.0), MARSHA, PMS, Richie

EDUCATION

Bachelor of Science (B.S.). In progress, Brindale University, Lakeland, CA
- Major: Recreation Administration

- Option: Resort and Lodging Management

RELATED COURSES

Communications
Foundations of Recreation Programming
Recreation Budget/Finance Management
Recreation Employment Law
Commercial Recreation and Tourism
Leisure Services Promotion
Resort and Lodging Operations
Management of Recreation
Leadership and Supervision in Recreation

PROFESSIONAL EXPERIENCE

- Sales Manager, Overnight Inn by Marion, Pleasant Valley, CA, (DATES)
- Manager in Training - Sales, Vestibule Inn by Marion, San Diego, CA, (DATES)
- Front Office Intern, Palm Springs Rediscovery Resort, (DATES)

SAMPLE ELECTRONIC OR SCANNABLE RÉSUMÉ (continued)

Résumé of Terri J. MacDonald – Page 2

PROFESSIONAL EXPERIENCE CONTINUED

- Patient Accounts Clerk, Spruce Memorial Hospital, North Calvert, CA, (DATES)
- Customer Service Representative, Daisy's Department Store, Eureka, CA (DATES)
- Inn Sitter and Housekeeper, Silverster House Bed and Breakfast, Finney, CA (DATES)

MANAGEMENT AND SALES EXPERIENCE

- Experience in hotel operations, including front office management, concierge, reservations, telecommunications, security, and night audits
- Established and monitored promotional budgets
- Recruited and trained sales representatives; met sales goals
- Developed and implemented market analysis
- Familiar with accounting principles and financial statements
- Developed brochure and advertising copy
- Provided customer service promoting customer loyalty and customer recovery

AWARDS

- Recreation Administration Student of the Year (YEAR)
- Soccer Sportsmanship Award (YEAR)

LEADERSHIP

- President, Eta Sigma Chi, Hospitality Management Honor Society, (YEARS)
- Vice-President, Associated Student Body, (YEARS)
- Activity Leadership at Dorothy B. Jackson Teen Program, (YEARS)
- Attended Marion Student Leadership Summit, (YEARS)
- Big Sister Mentor, Community Organization Volunteers in Education
- Member, Society of Leisure and Recreation

The Portfolio

Developing a portfolio, either in print format or electronic (e.g., web-based, CD-ROM), can be a boon to the candidate for an internship. The portfolio enables you to supplement your résumé by providing visual evidence of your abilities to a potential internship supervisor. Moreover, it allows you to present examples of your best work in a convenient and professional manner. Consider some of the following ways a portfolio might be useful, in conjunction with your résumé:

- Visual (eportfolio) evidence of programs or experiences that you have been involved in that relate to the present internship opportunity (i.e., raft guide-leadership skills, after school leader-programming skills, lifeguard-aquatic skills, event planner-programmatic skills, docent-interpretive skills, camp counselor-special need skills, seasonal ranger experiences, problem solving). Each of these examples might have moving visual samples linked to the experience listed on your résumé. Imagine a one-minute rafting visual on a Class IV-V river showing your leadership skills that could get a potential supervisor's attention.

- Concrete examples of both your academic and professional work. These examples can attest to your writing skills, organizational abilities, technological skills, and professional expertise. The more skills you can demonstrate through your portfolio, the more valuable you will be to a potential internship site. For example, a portfolio can allow you to demonstrate proficiency in a wide variety of computer software, such as PowerPoint, Excel, iMovie, Photoshop, Camtasia, etc.

- Projects related to the profession, such as business plans, park planning, budgets, marketing plans, and research projects can be effectively highlighted in a portfolio. You might include evidence of how you led a team of students through a project from beginning to end, including copies of television and newspaper coverage and letters of accomplishment from the agency or university faculty.

> Tip: If you elect to construct an eportfolio, a digital recorder should be one of your tools. The recorder can be used for documenting events, projects, and other items that could be included in a web-based or CD-ROM portfolio. Begin now to establish an ongoing, visual record of your professional involvement.

Agency supervisors are looking for ways to identify the best internship candidates, and portfolios are rapidly becoming the norm for assessing the capabilities of potential interns. Thus, the information in your portfolio needs to be up-to-date and representative of your best work. We suggest updating your portfolio every six months to one year. The following indicates what might be included in print-based portfolio:

- An appropriate storage (i.e., notebook, binder, plastic envelope)
- Cover page (your name, address, phone and cell number, e-mail, possible graphic)
- Typed letter of introduction (similar to a cover letter with no address)
- Typed résumé (on professional paper)
- Two to three letters of recommendation
- Three samples of your work
- A copy of your college transcripts (optional)
- Copies of your personal interests and achievements

An eportfolio should include most of the above components, and has the advantage of using sophisticated features (e.g., audio, video, interactive elements) to emphasize your professional assets and capabilities. If you use a web-based portfolio, be sure to include your site's address (URL) on your résumé. To see a few examples of eportfolios, check the links provided on p. 54.

Selecting Your References

It is never too early to ask for a reference letter. There are two types of references: professional and personal. One of the first things you should do is contact the person you want to write the reference letter; **never** use a person as a reference without first asking him or her for permission. Once you have received the approval the process begins. Remember to give the person writing the reference ample time to compose the letter. It is suggested that you give at least three weeks notice when asking someone to write a reference letter for you.

References may include:
- Present or past employers
- Faculty members (i.e., your teachers)
- Your academic advisor
- Professional mentors
- Athletic coaches
- "Character" references

The character reference is an old idea; however, it is still effective because it provides a different dimension than most of the other types of references. This is a reference that has watched you grow up and mature into the person you are today. Examples of character references include the spiritual leader at your place of worship, a parent of children for whom you were the babysitter, a neighbor, or parent of one of your childhood friends. These individuals know you and can attest to your personal character.

You should provide your references with:
- The name, title, and complete address of the agency contact
- Procedures for submitting each letter (e.g., direct to agency or to you, deadline for submission)
- A copy of your most recent résumé
- A copy of the internship position description
- Information regarding why you are interested in the internship
- What specific skills and/or qualities you want references to emphasize

You should keep an electronic copy of your reference list, as well as hard copy back-ups. You might also have additional references in mind, should your interviewer ask for more than those on your reference list. Asking your reference for a copy of the letter written in your behalf can also be a good idea. Thus, if you want additional (i.e., future) letters written by this person, it is a nice touch to provide a copy of the old reference letter so he or she does not need to "reinvent the wheel." Lastly, make sure you send a thank-you note to your reference.

A sample reference list is included on page 116.

Online and E-mail Applications

Online Applications

Many agencies are requiring that you complete an online application which may, or may not, require an attachement of your résumé. When completing an online application, it is best to follow the directions specifically. If the agency does not request your résumé or cover letter, do not send it. Following the instructions of the agency can be a first test regarding your potential success at the agency.

E-mail Applications

If you are requested to send your application via e-mail, here are some suggestions for making a good first impression:

1. Proofread your e-mail. Check your e-mail for grammar and spelling errors (do not trust spell check software). This is your opportunity to make an important first impression; your e-mails need to be professional and error-free.

2. Be brief. You may convert your cover letter to introduce yourself in your e-mail, but ensure that the cover letter is no more than three short paragraphs. If the job posting asks you to send an attachment, send your cover letter as an MSWord or PDF document. PDFs ensure that the formatting of your résumé is preserved. Many employers do not accept attachments. In these cases, paste your résumé into your e-mail message. Use a simple font and remove the fancy formatting. Send the message to yourself first to test that the formatting works. If everything looks good, resend to the employer.

3. Include a complete signature. Make sure that your signature includes your full name, address, phone number and e-mail address (ensure your e-mail address is professional or change it).

4. Create a subject line. Include the title of the position that your are hoping to obtain in the subject line of your e-mail.

Summary

The information in this chapter and the preceding one helped you to design the tools (i.e., cover letter and résumé) necessary for applying for an internship. Exercises and examples were provided for your use and information. Use these exercises and examples, plus your own knowledge, to develop the tools that will work best for you. Remember, these tools represent you, and are usually the first examples of your work that a potential internship supervisor sees. Make them represent the *best* you.

Now that you have prepared high-quality tools and have shown the best you, it is the potential internship supervisor's turn to evaluate how well you match his or her agency's needs. If all goes well, the next aspect of the internship process should be the interview. Chapter Six provides many excellent tips on how to be ready for that big day.

Chapter Six
The Interview

There is always one moment…when the door opens and lets the future in.—Graham Greene

When preparing for an internship, nothing causes more stress than the idea of going through an interview. If you are like most students, you do not have a lot of experience with interviews. Therefore, you have concerns about how to dress, how to act, what you might be asked, and what to say during an interview. This chapter will help you cope with these and other concerns prior to, during, and after the internship interview.

To prepare for an interview, you must:
- Develop the proper frame of mind
- Do your homework
- Practice, practice, practice

When participating in an interview, you should:
- Know the different types of interviews
- Display professionalism during the interview
- Follow up after the interview

Preparing for an Interview

Developing the Proper Frame of Mind

First, it is important to understand that an internship interview is a two-way process. You are, of course, being evaluated by the interviewer, but you are also evaluating whether this agency and agency supervisor are right for you. Recognizing that you are an equal participant in the interview process is essential—it will help give you confidence and ensure that you are in the proper frame of mind throughout the interview. Moreover, research has shown that many interviewers do not take the time to prepare properly for their interviews. If you have thoroughly prepared for your half of the interview, you will often have the advantage in an interview situation.

Chapter One (Self-Assessment) helped you develop positive self-talk. At this point, quickly review "Your Top 10 Assets" (p. 13). The foundation of a successful interview is to think positively and project a confident, professional image.

Doing Your Homework

Being successful during interviews does not just happen. It takes a lot of hard work to prepare for an interview, including attending to logistical concerns, reviewing data about the agency, reviewing your self-assessment, preparing answers to questions you might be asked, and preparing questions that you want to ask.

Logistical Concerns

There are many logistical things to keep in mind as you prepare for an interview. For example, you need to know exactly how to get to the interview site and how long it will take to get there. If the interview site is in a busy area, you should plan an alternative route in case of traffic delays. Additional logistical concerns include having an extra copy of your résumé to take with you, selecting and preparing the clothes you plan to wear, writing or calling to confirm the interview, preparing a portfolio, and making sure you have enough change for making a phone call or for parking. Also, if you have a cell phone, you must remember to turn it off before entering the interview situation. Some of these things may seem trivial, but overlooking a minor item can sometimes cause a major problem.

We suggest that you take the time to put logistical information in a checklist format. Thus, preliminary items will become routine, allowing you to concentrate on other aspects of the interview process (see *Interview Logistics Checklist*). Under pressure, everyone has a tendency to forget important things. Use the checklist as a reminder of what you need to do, as well as what you need to take with you to the interview. Also, remember to add necessary items as you identify them.

Most of the information on the checklist is self-explanatory, but a couple of logistical items should be discussed:

1. *Confirmation Letter or Call.* There are few experiences more embarrassing than arriving at an interview site at the wrong day or time. Therefore, a few days before your appointed interview, you should confirm the date, time, and location of your interview. This may be done by letter or, if you prefer, by phone. Confirming your appointment by phone also gives you the chance to ask for directions if needed and clarify parking arrangements.

2. *Practice Trip to Interview Location.* If you are not familiar with the location of your interview site, how to get there, or the traffic patterns in the area, we suggest you take a practice trip in advance of the interview date. It is essential to arrive on time for an interview; therefore, you need to know *exactly* where you are going and how long it will take you to get there. If heavy traffic may be a problem, be sure to do your practice trip at the same time of day as your interview. Also, be sure to practice your alternative route.

3. *The Portfolio.* If you have a print portfolio, you should consider taking it to the interview with you. You might offer your portfolio during the interview or even at the end of the interview; however, do *not* force the portfolio on the interviewer. Let him or her know that it exists and be ready to show it with pride. If you have developed a web-based portfolio, let the interviewer know about it and be sure to provide him or her with the URL for your portfolio. Return to the end of Chapter Five (The Résumé) for additional details about the portfolio.

4. *Review of Agency Data.* Chapter Three (Search and Research) helped you to identify ways to gather detailed information on potential internship agencies. Before an interview, it is essential to review this information. An interviewer will be impressed if you demonstrate knowledge of his or her agency. Also, reviewing agency data will help you to prepare insightful questions to use during the interview (see "Do you know?" below).

Do you know?

Prior to going on an interview, do you know the:

- Precise name of the agency (and department, if applicable)?
- Name (including spelling) and title of potential internship supervisor?
- Internship job description, if applicable?
- Programs and services offered by the agency/department?
- Demographics and size of population served?
- Size of the agency's professional staff?
- Organizational chart of the agency/department?
- Industry's trends that might affect the agency/department?
- Names and titles of alumni from your university working in the agency/department?

Interview Logistics Checklist

Contact Person:

_____

Agency Name, Address, and Phone Numbers:

_____

_____

_____

Part I. Advance Preparation

_____ Set date of interview
_____ Set time of interview
_____ Set location of interview
_____ Identify person to report to
_____ Write or call to confirm interview (including time/date/location)
_____ Secure map to interview location
_____ Determine best route to interview location
_____ Identify alternative route, if needed
_____ Take practice trip to interview location, if possible
_____ Check gas gauge on car before leaving
_____ Make extra copy of résumé
_____ Complete employment application, if needed
_____ Make extra copy of reference letters, if appropriate
_____ Prepare portfolio, if appropriate
_____ Select clothes and accessories (e.g., jewelry)
_____ Prepare clothes (e.g., cleaning, washing, pressing, shining shoes)
_____ Review your self-assessment of your personality traits and professional skills
_____ Prepare answers to potential interview questions regarding university requirements
_____ Review internship description, if available
_____ Turn off cell phone before interview

Part II. Things to Take

_____ Interviewer's name and phone number
_____ Change for parking
_____ Map or GPS to interview location (including precise address of location)
_____ Copy of résumé (plus reference letters and/or employment application, if appropriate)
_____ Portfolio (if appropriate)
_____ Agency brochures, interview notes (to review prior to interview)

5. *Self-Assessment Review.* Chapter One (Self-Assessment) provided information and exercises to help you to understand yourself more thoroughly. The interview gives you a chance to put this information into action. One of the things interviewers will look for during an interview is whether or not you understand yourself and your own capabilities. Reviewing the forms in Chapter One is excellent preparation for an interview.

6. *Preparation of Answers to Potential Questions.* Usually you will not know in advance the questions that will be asked during your interview. Nevertheless, you *can* prepare for interview questions. One way is to check with your classmates. Have any of them interviewed with the agency? If so, ask for their advice, with particular attention to questions they were asked during the interview. One question most internship interviewers ask is, "What does your university expect from your agency supervisor?" Be sure that you know your university's expectations regarding all requirements such as paperwork, interns' evaluations, and conferences with faculty members. You should also carefully review questions that are commonly asked during internship interviews and prepare answers to as many as possible.

Exercise Time

Exercise 6.1 provides a list of 30 interview questions frequently asked of potential interns. Taking the time now to answer each of these questions may relieve you of a great deal of stress and tension later. Review each question and write down your answer in the space provided. Be thorough, but concise. After you have finished writing down your answers, give some thought to Weird Questions You Might Be Asked, Other Potential Questions, and Situational Questions listed at the end of Exercise 6.1.

Exercise 6.1: Internship Interview Questions

The following are questions frequently asked of interns during an interview. Read each question, then use the space provided to formulate your answer. The purpose of this exercise is not to have you memorize your answers; rather, it is to help you think through your responses in advance. Then, if one of these questions is asked during your interview, you will be able to respond in a relaxed and natural manner. Remember to keep your answers brief but thorough.

1. What are your short-term and long-term goals, and how are you preparing to reach them?

_____

_____

_____

2. Why did you choose this career, and what do you want to gain from it?

_____

_____

_____

3. What do you consider to be your greatest strengths and weaknesses?

_____

_____

_____

4. What experiences do you have with people from diverse ethnic and religious backgrounds?

_____

_____

_____

5. If we called one of your references, what would he or she say about you?

_____

_____

_____

6. What has been your biggest disappointment at work?

_____

_____

_____

7. Why should I take you as an intern?

_____

_____

_____

8. How well do you function under pressure? Provide examples.

_____

_____

_____

9. What things have you learned in school that will help you as an intern?

_____

_____

_____

10. Why did you decide to seek an internship with this agency?

_____

_____

_____

11. If you came with a warning label, what would it say? Why?

_____

_____

_____

12. Describe a mistake you have made in your life and tell me what you learned from it?

_____

_____

_____

13. How do you define success?

_____

_____

_____

14. What qualities do you think a good internship supervisor should have?

_____

_____

_____

15. What qualities do you think a good intern should have?

_____

_____

_____

16. What are you doing to keep up to date with your field?

_____

_____

_____

17. Describe a problem that you have faced and tell me how you solved it. What did you learn from this experience?

_____

_____

_____

18. How are your written communication skills?

_____

_____

_____

19. Why do you feel you are qualified for an internship position?

_____

_____

_____

20. What are the three most important things you have learned from your formal education?

_____

_____

_____

21. What are your greatest concerns about starting your internship?

_____

_____

_____

22. Do your grades show your true potential? If not, why not?

_____

_____

_____

23. What two or three accomplishments have given you the most satisfaction?

_____

_____

_____

24. Name two or three things most important to you in selecting your internship site?

_____

_____

_____

_____

25. What experiences do you have speaking before groups and how well did you perform?

_____

_____

_____

26. What do you find most satisfying in a job?

_____

_____

_____

27. What experiences do you have with computers?

_____

_____

_____

28. Would you describe yourself as an ethical person? If so, why?

_____

_____

_____

29. Describe a discipline problem you have had to handle. How did you deal with it?

_____

_____

_____

30. What motivates you to put forth your greatest effort?

_____

_____

_____

Weird Questions You Might Be Asked

Sometimes interviewers will ask odd questions to try to throw you off or test your responses to the unexpected. Here are some weird questions that have actually been asked of our students:

- If you were a fruit (or animal), what kind of fruit (animal) would you be?
- What is your favorite food? Why?
- What color tablecloth would you put on your dinner table for a party?
- If Hollywood was to make a movie of your life, which actor or actress would you choose to portray you?
- What is your favorite song (or movie)?
- If you could be a superhero, what would you want your super power(s) to be?
- If you won ten million dollars in the lottery, what would you do with the money?

Other Potential Questions

- Describe how you were able to demonstrate teamwork at school or at your last job.
- What does the word "service" mean to you?
- Have you had personal experience with persons who have physical or mental disabilities? Describe them.
- Why did you select (your university)?
- What organizations do you belong to?
- What has been your most interesting job? Why?
- What has been your least interesting job? Why?
- If you were me, would you select yourself for this internship? Why?
- What skills do you think are crucial for an intern to possess?
- What do you know about this agency?
- Do you like to travel? Why?
- What do you see yourself doing five years from now?
- What are your hobbies and interests?
- What types of books do you read for pleasure? Tell me about one of them.
- What techniques do you use to motivate others?
- What actions would you take to build positive relationships with the media?
- What implications does the Americans with Disabilities Act have for the way you offer programs?

Situational Questions

You should also be prepared to answer situational questions (i.e., those questions where you are given a situation and asked to react to it). Remember, however, that most agencies already have policies and procedures set up for many routine situations. If you think a policy might exist, consider prefacing your answer by saying, "If the agency has an established policy for handling this situation, I would follow it. If not, I would…" The following are some examples of situational questions:

- You have worked hard preparing a promotional brochure for the agency, but another intern shows it to your supervisor and takes credit for your work. What would you do?

- You take a group of individuals with head injuries on a community outing. During the trip, one of your clients makes an inappropriate sexual advance toward you. How would you react to the advance and what would you do after returning to the agency?

- You are working on a project with two other interns. As the project progresses, you become aware that one of the interns is violating company policy by taking agency materials for personal use. What would you do?

- Over time, you become convinced that a child in one of your recreation programs is the victim of child abuse. Should you do anything about your suspicions? If so, what?

- You are leading an activity for teenagers in our nature center. During the session, you hear one of the teenagers make a racist remark. The purpose of your session is environmental awareness, not race relations, and no members of the racial group in question are present. What, if anything, should you do?

Preparing Questions You Want to Ask

As mentioned previously, the internship interview is a two-way process. Not only does the interviewer need to decide if the agency wants you as an intern, but you have to decide if this agency offers the internship experience you want. You should not leave the interview without knowing the answers to the following questions:

- Who will be your direct supervisor?

- Has the agency had interns before?

- Has your direct supervisor had experience supervising interns?

- What work schedule will you be expected to maintain (days/hours)?

- What will be your primary duties and responsibilities?

- What will be the nature of your orientation upon arrival?

- What are the possibilities of job opportunities with the agency (only if you hope to work there after graduation)?

- Do interns receive a stipend or salary (only if important to selection of your internship agency)?

- Does the agency have any special requirements or policies regarding interns (e.g., attire, policies on visitors)?

- Can you meet your educational goals as an intern with the agency?

- How are interns evaluated?

- When will a decision about your internship application be made, and how it will be communicated to you?

- If you will be seeking certification in therapeutic recreation (TR), will your internship responsibilities qualify you for taking the certifying examination? Also, are additional full-time, certified persons available in case your immediate supervisor leaves the agency for any reason during your internship? (For additional information on TR certification, contact the National Council for Therapeutic Recreation Certification; see Appendix B).

Generally, most of the above information will be given to you without asking. If, however, some of these items are not covered by your interviewer, you must be prepared to ask questions. When asking questions, it is important to emphasize aspects of the internship that are important to your educational goals and career development. Do *not* ask trivial questions or questions that have obvious answers. Use the above list, plus other information that you want to learn during the interview, to develop a list of questions that you might ask during your interview.

Exercise Time

Use Exercise 6.2 to write down the questions you want to ask the interviewer.

Exercise 6.2: Questions to Ask an Interviewer

List 10 questions that you might ask an interviewer. Arrange your questions from most important (#1) to least important (#10).

Question #1: _____

_____

_____

_____

Question #2: _____

_____

_____

_____

Question #3: _____

_____

_____

_____

Question #4: _____

_____

_____

_____

Question #5: _____

_____

_____

_____

Question #6: _____

_____

_____

_____

Question #7: _____

_____

_____

_____

Question #8: _____

_____

_____

_____

Question #9: _____

_____

_____

_____

Question #10: _____

_____

_____

_____

Practice, Practice, Practice

The final step in preparing for an internship interview is to practice your interviewing skills…over and over again. Like most skills, answering questions in an interview situation does not come naturally. It takes practice to learn how to relax and answer difficult questions with ease and confidence. It takes practice to learn how to ask important questions of an interviewer without sounding either defensive or aggressive. It also takes practice to eliminate annoying mannerisms or distracting movements during an interview situation.

But, exactly how can you practice your interviewing skills? One of the most effective ways is to participate in "mock" interviews. Start by asking a friend or relative to interview you. Pretend you are in a real interview situation and have the friend or relative ask you questions from Exercise 6.1. This will give you practice in verbalizing answers that you have already put on paper. Moreover, it will enable you to start practicing your interviewing skills in a very nonthreatening environment. If possible, record your mock interview, then sit down and discuss what things you did well and what areas still need work. Pay particular attention to such things as distracting mannerisms, poor grammar, and verbal fillers (e.g., "ums").

Next, ask a *different* friend or relative to interview you, only this time have him or her develop the questions. This may give you practice in responding to questions you have not thought about before. Again, after the mock interview is over, process the interview to identify your strengths and weaknesses. If the staff members at your university's career development center conduct mock interviews, also interview with them and have them evaluate your skills. Although these individuals may not have in-depth knowledge about recreation and leisure services, they are experts in interviewing techniques.

Finally, after you feel comfortable with your interviewing skills, it is time to participate in the real thing—an internship interview. If you have a "first choice" agency, we suggest that you *not* interview with this agency until you have interviewed at one or two other potential agencies. Thus, by the time you interview at the agency you want most, your interviewing skills should be at their peak.

Participating in an Interview

Types of Internship Interviews

Face-to-Face Interviews

It is difficult to predict exactly how an internship interview will be conducted. Most of the time, internship interviews are face-to-face and one-to-one; however, sometimes more than one staff member will interview you. Generally, an interviewer will want to show you around the agency and familiarize you with its departments and services. This may take place before or after a formal questioning period; however, important interview questions may also be asked *while* you are being shown around the agency. Remember you are applying for an internship, not a full-time job. Try to relax and be prepared for any type of interview.

Sometimes interviewers are so anxious to have student interns that they do not even conduct a formal interview. Rather, they use the interview time to sell their agency to the student. If this happens to you, do not forget that *you* have lots of questions that need to be answered. Even if someone chooses not to interview you, make sure you still get your questions answered.

If a formal interview is held, it will usually go through three stages:

1. *Breaking the Ice.* In this stage, the interviewer will generally try to make you comfortable in the interview situation. Nonthreatening topics are usually discussed, such as the weather, local sports, or your university. If other interviewers are present, they will usually be introduced and their roles explained during this stage.

2. *Inquiry.* This is the stage where the interviewer asks specific questions of you. Generally, these questions are designed to find out what kind of a person you are and what kind of an intern you will be. Provided you have done a good job of preparing, this stage should not produce anxiety for you. This is also the stage where you ask your questions of the interviewer.

3. *Conclusion.* At this stage, the interviewer controls the ending of the interview and lets you know what happens next (e.g., when a decision will be made and how you will be notified). It also provides a final chance for either you or the interviewer to get clarification on any aspect of the interview process.

On rare occasions, a second internship interview is held. This requires a potential intern to return for another interview. This second interview is generally more in-depth than the first one, and usually means that there is stiff competition for an internship position. Situational questions (see Exercise 6.1, p. 143) are sometimes saved for a second interview.

Telephone Interviews

Internship interviews, unlike most job interviews, are sometimes conducted by telephone. Often, a student who wishes to do his or her internship a great distance from school and home cannot afford the time or expense to travel to an agency's location just for an interview. Thus, it becomes necessary to conduct a telephone interview. Telephone interviews may seem to be less threatening than face-to-face interviews because the student's concerns about proper attire, distracting mannerisms, and other one-on-one situations are eliminated. However, telephone interviews do not allow a student to demonstrate his or her professionalism and enthusiasm through such details as proper dress and good use of nonverbal communication. Preparation is critical. Some students lay out index cards with potential interview questions and keyword answers on a coffee table when taking the call. Voice quality, voice inflection, grammar, and word usage are paramount in a telephone interview. Moreover, the student often must be very assertive to ensure that all of his or her questions are answered. Telephone interviews may be expedient, but they are often as stressful as face-to-face interviews and have significant disadvantages. We *strongly* urge you to do your interviews in-person, if possible, because you will learn more about a potential agency and supervisor during a face-to-face interview. Also, telephone interviews do *not* help to prepare you for the job interviews that lie ahead.

Online Interviews

Some agency professionals are beginning to use online tools to conduct interviews at a distance. For example, use of Skype, iChat, and similar programs are increasingly becoming popular interviewing strategies. If you know that you are going to be interviewed online where you are visible to the interviewer, preparation is much the same as for the face-to-face interview. Critically important, however, is that you dedicate the time to download and become familiar with the online tool that is to be utilized for the interview. For example, ensuring that you have a working camera and microphone, and performing audio and video checks will be necessary. It is also strongly suggested that you practice communications with another student or friend to ensure that the technology will not negatively impact the interview process.

Displaying Professionalism During Internship Interviews

The interview is crucial because it is usually the first time the potential employer has a chance to "meet" you. It is also the primary means for agency personnel to answer crucial questions about you and your professional abilities. These questions include:

- Do you present a positive, professional image?
- Are you a self-motivated person?
- Do you communicate well verbally?
- Do you have good command of your area of specialization?
- Do you understand yourself?
- Can you state four or five examples of your skills and abilities?
- Are you knowledgeable about the agency?
- Can you think clearly under pressure?
- Are you patient and tactful?

- Are you a mature person?
- Do you have the right attitude to be an intern with the agency?

Extensive preparation helps to ensure that your interviewer will answer "yes" to many of these questions; however, the following are other important things to keep in mind when you participate in an interview.

Appearance and Grooming

For some students, one appealing characteristic of the recreation and parks profession is that it is often not bound by the traditional "office attire" guidelines and regulations of corporate America. Many interns will go on to work in employment settings that allow a wide range of freedom in appropriate attire. As future managers and practitioners, we appreciate and value this type of flexibility. However, regardless of the type of clothing you will wear on the job, you will want to dress "up" for your internship interview.

What does it mean to dress "up" for an interview? In a nutshell, it means selecting clothing, accessories, and adornments (jewelry) in such a way as to represent you as a professional and in the best light possible. When it comes to interviewing for a professional internship, you want to dress for the position you want (as a professional), not for the position you have (as a student). Research documents that negative impressions made during an interview may bring with them negative outcomes for the interviewee. Dressing professionally can help prevent negative initial impressions. It will also send a message to your interviewer that you respect the position, as well as the opportunity to interview for the internship.

Select your clothes well in advance of the interview date, and check them carefully for neatness, cleanliness, and fit the night before. If you do not have an "eye" for colors and styles, have a knowledgeable friend or relative help you select your interview attire. It is important to be relaxed and comfortable during the interview, so wear clothing that helps you feel that way. Also, avoid wearing anything into the interview that might distract you or your interviewer (e.g., a tie that is too "loud" or tied too tightly; too much makeup, perfume, or aftershave; excess jewelry).

Although the above generalities are important starting points for preparing for an interview, the following two points may also help you make the right attire selection for you as an individual:

1. **Stay true to yourself.** Dressing up for an interview does not mean you relinquish your freedom of expression. The important point is to stay true to who you are, while also dressing professionally. For example, if you are a person who is most comfortable wearing bright and vibrant colors (as opposed to traditional black, blues, and grays), then wear colors you enjoy. However, you should consider wearing shades of these colors that are muted (remember, you do not want to distract your interviewer). Also, if you are a woman who does not feel comfortable in a skirt, by all means, wear slacks. Remember, it is not whether you are wearing a skirt or slacks, it is the appearance of the skirt or slacks that is critical (i.e., clean, pressed, and well-fitted clothing).

2. **Know the interview situation.** Let the interview situation "guide" your clothing choices. For example, if you are going to serve as an adventure guide, you might choose to wear clean, pressed slacks and shirt (men, you might add a tasteful tie). Wearing a two-piece navy pinstriped suit to this type of situation may be out of context. On the other hand, if you are interviewing for an internship in a "business" environment, selecting more traditional interview attire may be in order. In this situation, a suit (slacks or skirt) will most likely be the best choice. It is likely that the interviewer will be looking at your appearance and considering it in a context of the agency he or she represents.

Confidence and Enthusiasm

From the moment you walk into your interview, you need to let your interviewer know that you have confidence in your abilities and enthusiasm for doing an internship with the agency. First, and foremost, relax as you approach the interview situation. Greet everyone you meet with a warm, energetic smile and a positive greeting (e.g., "I've been looking forward to this interview."). If a handshake is appropriate, be sure to offer a firm one. Respond to questions directly and concisely, but be certain to answer them completely. Avoid yes/no responses, one-word answers, and long, rambling responses. Be aware of your pace of speech to assure that it is neither too fast nor too slow. Be sure that your answers demonstrate genuine interest in the agency and its services. Moreover, display confidence that as an intern you will be an asset to the agency.

Sincerity

It is essential that your interviewer get to know the real you. If you try to act like someone else during an interview, you will probably be perceived as insincere. Rather, just relax and act naturally. If something funny happens, laugh with your interviewer. If you are describing an emotional experience, show a little of your emotion. You want your interviewer to know that you are both professional and personable.

Nonverbal Communication

People say a lot about themselves without even opening their mouths. The way they sit or the way they walk tells people how they feel about themselves and others. Research indicates that such nonverbal communication may be as important, and possibly more important, than verbal communication. Let people know you have confidence in yourself by maintaining eye contact with them during the interview. Maintain an upright, but not stiff, posture with just a little forward lean. Acknowledge what others say with a nod, confirming that you are carefully listening to them. Also, attending to their nonverbal communication will help you respond appropriately during the interview.

Concentration and Active Listening

Interviewing takes intense concentration and active listening skills. Attend carefully to what is said to you during the interview. It is embarrassing to ask a question that has already been answered by an interviewer. Also, concentrate intensely on questions that you are asked. If you do not understand a question, it is perfectly acceptable to ask for clarification; however, if you do not hear a question, an interviewer may have doubts about your listening skills.

Habits and Mannerisms

Do you have any bad habits or annoying mannerisms that may affect your interviews, such as twisting your hair, playing with jewelry, tapping a pencil or pen, or fidgeting? Habits are things you have learned, and you can eliminate them only through relearning or retraining. The first step toward eliminating these habits is to identify them during your mock interviews. Then practice your interviewing skills, concentrating on leaving out any bad habits or annoying mannerisms.

Positive Attitude

Agency supervisors like to have student interns who are upbeat and positive in their approach to school, work, and life. Be sure that your interview reflects a positive outlook. Avoid making negative or sarcastic statements about your university or previous employment. If a question requires you to say something negative (e.g., "What do you like least about your previous job?"), try to have your response include positive aspects (e.g., "We did not have a large enough budget to put all of our programming ideas into action."). As stated by Dana May Casperson, "Your attitude is evident in your body language, how you complete tasks, your attention to detail, your consideration of those around you, how you take care of yourself, and in your general approach to life."

Promptness

Arriving to an interview on time demonstrates that you are a reliable person who can be counted on. We suggest that you plan to arrive at the facility at least 15 minutes early, but do *not* report to the receptionist until just before the appointment time. Use the extra time to go over information on the agency, review your answers to potential questions, and if necessary stop at the restroom.

Nervousness and Mistakes

Despite attempts to relax and display confidence, it is natural to be nervous during an internship interview. Good interviewers understand this, and they won't judge you harshly if you appear a little nervous or make a mistake during the interview. If this happens, feel free to admit your nervousness, take a second to relax and restore your confidence, then continue with the interview. Not getting flustered by nervousness or a mistake demonstrates to an interviewer that you respond well under pressure.

Control

During the interview, it is important to remember that the interviewer is in control. Allow him or her to take the lead. In an interview, it is important not to come across as argumentative, pushy, or overconfident. Allowing the interviewer to set the tone and pace of an interview lets him or her know that you understand when *not* to assert yourself. The interviewer also decides how and when to conclude the interview. However, remember that you do need to assert yourself at the end of the interview if all of your questions/concerns have not been addressed.

Legal Considerations

Interviewers usually know what questions can be asked of potential interns, as well as what questions cannot be asked legally. You, too, should be aware of what questions an interviewer is not allowed to ask you. This can be very important if, for any reason, you believe your answers to illegal questions resulted in discrimination against you. To help you, we suggest you visit the following website: http://www.iseek.org/jobs/legalquestions.html

In addition to knowing what questions are illegal, you should also consider how you would respond to these questions. In general, most experts suggest one of three responses. These include:

1. If you are completely comfortable providing the information requested, just answer the question. This approach has the least risk of making the interviewer respond defensively, but it also carries the risk of discrimination based upon your answer.

2. If a question is offensive to you or you have reservations about the interviewer's motivation, you can refuse to answer the question. In so doing, you should state that the question does not appear to be legal or is unrelated to the functions of the internship position. This approach, of course, risks offending the interviewer, but may be an appropriate response if a question is blatantly offensive.

3. A compromise between the two alternatives above is to respond to the intent of an illegal question. For example, the interviewer might ask "how old are you," (illegal question) when he or she really wants to ensure that you are over 18 years of age (legal question if 18 is the minimum age for the internship). Your response might be, "I assume you are wondering if am over the internship's minimum age of 18. The answer is yes."

Ultimately, your response to an illegal question will vary with the situation, including the nature of the interview and your rapport with the interviewer. For additional information on this topic, we suggest you use a search engine (e.g., Google) to find sites with detailed suggestions for responding to illegal questions. Simply search on "How to Handle Illegal Interview Questions."

Conclusion

At the end of the interview, be sure to smile and thank everyone associated with the interview, including the receptionist. Final impressions, like first impressions, tend to be lasting ones.

Following Up after an Interview

Yogi Berra is credited with saying, "It ain't over 'til it's over." An internship interview is not even over when it appears to be over. You still need to follow up after the actual interview is complete, including correspondence with your interviewer, self-evaluation, and agency assessment.

Correspondence

It is generally considered good interview etiquette to write a *brief* thank-you letter expressing your appreciation for the interview. This letter also gives you the chance to reemphasize your enthusiasm for the agency's programs and services, and to restate how much you hope to learn during an internship with the agency. Finally, this letter allows you to add any information you may have forgotten to convey during the interview. Be sure to send your thank-you letter as soon as possible after the interview. Also, if you promised to send additional information (e.g., references, examples of your writing) to the interviewer, be sure to include that information with your thank-you letter. See the sample thank-you letters for good examples of correspondence to write following face-to-face interviews.

Generally, print thank-you letters are preferred over e-mail correspondence; however, e-mail follow-up correspondence is appropriate if the interviewer suggested it as a good way to communicate or stay in touch. If you use e-mail make sure that your e-mail address and writing style are professional. E-mail is easy, so many people are too casual with this form of communication. All of your communication with a potential internship site must be professional.

Regardless of what type of thank-you correspondence you use (i.e., print or e-mail), be sure you communicate your appreciation to the interviewer. It has been estimated that only 36% of job seekers send thank-you notes, yet over 75% of executives think that such notes are an important aspect of the hiring process (*Centre Daily Times,* September 9, 2007, p. D9).

Phone Follow-up

Another way to convey your appreciation to an interviewer is by telephone or cell phone. This is a good way to show your continued enthusiasm and commitment to the internship position for which you have applied. Telephone calls, including voice mail messages, should be rather short and to the point. Therefore, you need to be well-prepared before you make the call. Practice what you want to say and how you want to say it. Be energetic, friendly, and factual. If you leave a voice mail message with a call-back number, be sure to pronounce your name clearly and state your telephone or cell phone number at the beginning and again at the end of your message. Remember to say the numbers slowly to allow time for the interviewer to write them down.

Self-Evaluation

Your follow-up should also include a self-evaluation of your interview performance. To conduct your self-evaluation, first review the information in Displaying Professionalism, then answer the following questions:
- Was your physical appearance appropriate? Do you feel you gave the impression of a well-groomed, healthy individual?
- Did you speak clearly, distinctly, and refrain from using inappropriate words such as *yeah, nope, and-uh, um, aahhh, like, you know,* or *anyways*?
- Were your answers direct, clear, and concise? Do you feel they were understood by the interviewer(s)?
- Did you use effective nonverbal communication?
- Were you self-confident, open, and at ease in your responses?

- Did you display enthusiasm for the agency and its services?
- What do you feel were your strong points or strengths during the interview?
- What do you feel were your weaknesses, and what steps will you take to improve upon them during future interviews?
- How would you rate your overall performance?

Agency and Supervisor Assessment

In addition to evaluating your performance during the interview, you also need to assess whether the interview revealed any new information about the agency or your potential supervisor. Pay particular attention to the interviewer's answers to important questions you asked during the interview (see Exercise 6.2, p. 151). If you met the person who is to supervise you, assess your comfort level with him or her. The box on p. 163, entitled *Characteristics of a Good Employer*, provides attributes to consider. Then, ask yourself, "Do I still feel that this agency and supervisor will help me meet my educational and career goals?" If the answer is "no," eliminate this agency from consideration and continue your internship search. If the answer is "yes," this agency should be considered when you make your final internship placement decision (Chapter Seven).

SAMPLE THANK-YOU LETTER #1

DATE of Typing

Ms. Patricia Lawson, CTRS
Director of Therapeutic Recreation
Marabelle State Hospital
4800 Tennison Road
Bridgewater, CT 00006

Dear Ms. Lawson:

Thank you for taking the time to interview me for an internship position at Marabelle State Hospital. I was extremely impressed with both the facilities at the hospital and your progressive Therapeutic Recreation program.

As you know, my career goal is to be a Certified Therapeutic Recreation Specialist working with persons who have psychological disorders. My visit to Marabelle State Hospital has reaffirmed this goal, and I am excited about the possibility of doing an internship under your supervision.

During the interview, you requested that I send you a sample of my writing. Enclosed is a copy of a paper I wrote entitled "Leisure Education for Persons with Addictive Disorders." This paper was written last semester for REC 479 (Issues and Trends in Therapeutic Recreation).

Thank you again for the interview, and I look forward to hearing from you soon.

Sincerely,

Betty Jean Tearney
34 Rennie Way
Storrs, CT 60000
(000) 497-0000

Enclosure

SAMPLE THANK-YOU LETTER #2

143 Hartswick Ave.
Tallahassee, FL 33333
(000) 322-1794

DATE of Typing

Mr. Terrance Brown
Golf Professional
Liberty Golf Club and Resort
Golf Club Lane
Sunnydale, FL 34444

Dear Mr. Brown:

I enjoyed meeting you last Thursday, and appreciate your interviewing me for an internship position at Liberty Golf Club and Resort. I especially want to thank you for providing me with an extensive tour of your impressive facilities.

During the interview, you expressed interest in knowing more about New Venture Country Club in New Orleans, where my parents are members. Enclosed is an informational brochure on New Venture. David Shank, New Venture's teaching professional, requested that you call him if you want additional information on the club.

Once again, thank you for the interview and tour. I look forward to hearing from you as soon as a decision is made regarding the internship position.

Sincerely,

Jean Broussard

Enclosure

-YOU LETTER #3

SAM

)1 Lincoln Avenue
stchester, MO 65119
00) 552-9003

DATE of Typing

Mr. Lawrence E. Preston
Resources Unlimited
14 West End Road
Columbia, MO 65203

Dear Mr. Preston:

Thank you very much for your taking the time to interview me for an internship position with Resources Unlimited. I especially appreciated the tour of your agency, which not only gave me the chance to meet many of your staff members, but also provided me with insight into Resources Unlimited's organizational structure. It was clear from my visit that Resources Unlimited would be an excellent internship opportunity for any student.

It was my understanding from the interview that you hope to finalize your internship offerings within the next two or three weeks. I will look forward to hearing from you then. In the meantime, should you have additional questions or desire more information, please feel free to contact me.

Thanks again for the interview and for the courtesy you and your entire staff extended to me.

Sincerely,

Thomas Tankar

Characteristics of a Good Employer

Open to change	Patient	Fair
Organized	High expectations	Observant
Persistent	Problem solver	Trustworthy
Consistent	Personable	Accepting
Professional	Punctual	Provides feedback
Gives constructive advice	Receptive to new ideas	Understanding
Acknowledges others	Flexible	Communicative
Delegates	Respectful	Risk taker
Optimistic	Appreciative	Progressive
Approachable	Realistic	Motivating
Thoughtful	Considerate	Reliable
Informative	Focused	Provides challenges
Encouraging	Supportive	Loyal
Dependable	Sets goals	Creative
Ethical	Sensitive	Displays sense of humor
Innovative	Intelligent	Leader
Adaptable	Trusting	

Handling Rejection

No matter how qualified you are, you may not be offered every internship for which you apply. It is important not to take rejection personally. Agency interviewers are seeking a specific set of skills that match their agency's needs; thus, the decision not to offer you an internship has nothing to do with your worth as a human being or your potential as an intern. Simply put, your skills and abilities may not be a good match with the requirements of the agency's internship.

If you are turned down, give consideration to following up by phone with your interviewer. It may seem awkward to ask why you were turned down, but the answers may help you understand how you were perceived during the interview process. This information can be very helpful as you prepare for future interviews. If you do ask why you were not selected, it is essential to do so in a sincere, respectful, and professional manner. Following up with an interviewer after rejection will demonstrate your interest in improving your interview skills, and it will keep your name in the interviewer's mind should another internship opening occur. As Lindsey Olson of the recruiting agency Paradigm Staffing stated, "Today's rejection can be tomorrow's offer letter" (*Centre Daily Times,* March 4, 2007, p. D7).

Summary

All the work you have done up to this point has led to the interview. An internship interview is a two-way process that provides information to both the interviewer and you. This chapter has assisted you in identifying areas to consider and practice before entering through your interviewer's doors. If you prepare carefully and thoroughly, you will be able to give your best effort throughout the interview process. Hopefully, your interviews will lead to one or more internship offers. Then, all that remains is for you to make your final decision. The next chapter will help to prepare you for making that decision.

Chapter Seven
Selection and Final Planning

Life is either a daring adventure or nothing at all.—Helen Keller

Following your internship interviews, if all went well, you should have more than one internship offer to consider. It is now time to select the agency that best meets your academic, professional, and personal needs. Sometimes the choice is obvious because one agency's internship program is ideal for your academic needs and future direction. Often, however, the choice is neither obvious nor easy to make.

This chapter will help you to:

- Organize your thoughts to select the best internship agency for *you*
- Notify agencies of your selection
- Plan for your internship experience

Making Your Selection

Many times, students who have received more than one internship offer will ask for help in making their selection. Although you *should* seek information from friends, relatives, and faculty members, remember that the final selection is up to you. The exercises in this manual, plus your interviews, have provided the information you need to make your final agency selection. If you are having trouble deciding which agency is best for you, answering the following questions will help:

If I did my internship at (*name of agency*), would I be able to

1. Refine and acquire professional skills important to my career (see Exercise 1.3)?
2. Do the type of work I enjoy most (see Exercise 2.1)?
3. Gain experience in the kind of professional position I ultimately want to have (see Exercise 2.1 and Exercise 2.3)?
4. Meet my internship goals (see Exercise 2.2)?
5. Meet my most important internship needs and preferences (see Exercise 3.3)?
6. Feel comfortable working with the people I met during my interview?

Exercise Time

 After answering these questions, does one agency stand out by meeting the criteria that are most important to you? If so, your choice should be easy. If not, complete the Internship Agency Evaluation Form (Exercise 7.1; photocopy as needed depending on the number of agencies you are comparing). By listing the pros and cons of each agency, your decision will be easier to make.

Exercise 7.1: Internship Agency Evaluation Form

Take some time to identify the pros and cons of doing an internship with the following agency. Then, compare this list with the pros and cons offered by other agencies you are considering. This comparison will help you decide which agency offers you the best internship.

Name of Agency _____

PROS	CONS
1. _____	1. _____
2. _____	2. _____
3. _____	3. _____
4. _____	4. _____
5. _____	5. _____
6. _____	6. _____
7. _____	7. _____
8. _____	8. _____
9. _____	9. _____
10. _____	10. _____
11. _____	11. _____
12. _____	12. _____
13. _____	13. _____
14. _____	14. _____
15. _____	15. _____
16. _____	16. _____
17. _____	17. _____
18. _____	18. _____
19. _____	19. _____
20. _____	20. _____
21. _____	21. _____
22. _____	22. _____
23. _____	23. _____
24. _____	24. _____

Your internship agency selection is *very* important to your professional career, so take your time. *Some Desirable Characteristics of an Internship Agency* provides additional considerations to assist with your decision. Consult with others, consider all of the previous information, and select the agency that offers you the best possible internship.

Notification of Selection

Once you have made your selection, you need to communicate your intentions to all agencies with which you interviewed. First, if you do not have your offer in writing, telephone your first choice agency and confirm the offer. Let appropriate agency personnel know that you appreciate being selected and tell them you plan to accept. You should also confirm important information at this time, such as pay or stipend, work responsibilities, starting date, and length of internship. Then, write an acceptance letter confirming your selection, expressing your excitement about the internship, and confirming important information. Sample acceptance letters follow.

After you have confirmed your selection with your internship agency, you need to notify other agencies that you will not be doing your internship with them. Even if you notify them by telephone, you should send a letter thanking them for their consideration and explaining your decision. This is often a difficult letter to write, but it is very important. Sending a well-written letter that declines an internship will demonstrate your professionalism and keep your options open for future employment with each agency. Sample letters declining an internship follow.

Some Desirable Characteristics of an Internship Agency

- Provides an internship experience that helps a student gain an understanding and appreciation of the role, duties, and responsibilities of a full-time employee
- Offers a flexible internship program tailored to meet the learning objectives of the student
- Has personnel with the necessary education, training, and experience to give appropriate supervision to student interns
- Provides the student with a personnel manual, including guidelines for the student engaged in an internship
- Provides a thorough orientation
- Assists each student, as well as his or her advisor, in discovering the student's strengths and weaknesses as a pre-professional
- Helps the student to understand the professional nature of his or her vocation
- Has an active, balanced, and ongoing training program for staff and interns
- Offers administrative and supervisory programs that are sound and effective
- Gives a supervisor sufficient time to provide high-quality supervision for student interns
- Provides periodic evaluations (verbal and written) of student involvement and performance

SAMPLE ACCEPTANCE LETTER #1

DATE of Typing

Ms. Patricia Lawson, CTRS
Director of Therapeutic Recreation
Marabelle State Hospital
4800 Tennison Road
Bridgewater, CT 06452

Dear Ms. Lawson:

I am pleased to accept your offer of an internship in Therapeutic Recreation at Marabelle State Hospital. After visiting your facility in March, I knew that your program was ideally suited to my professional interests, and I am very excited about the learning opportunities available to me.

As I mentioned during our phone conversation, my internship is scheduled to begin on May 6 and end on August 5. It is my understanding that I will work 40 hours per week, receive a stipend of $100 per week, and be supervised by Mr. Thomas Calloway, CTRS. I enjoyed meeting Tom during my visit, and look forward to learning from him.

Thank you for offering me an internship with your program, and I look forward to seeing you in May.

Sincerely,

Betty Jean Tearney
34 Rennie Way
Storrs, CT 06268
(000) 497-2874

SAMPLE ACCEPTANCE LETTER #2

DATE of Typing

Mr. William James
Wild Adventures, Inc.
100 Adventures Lane
Omaha, NE 79001

Dear Mr. James:

Thank you for offering me an internship position with Wild Adventures, Inc. As I indicated during my interview, Wild Adventures provides the type of learning environment I am seeking; therefore, I enthusiastically accept your offer.

I hope to begin my 12-week internship on June 3, but will call you within the next two weeks to confirm dates and make other necessary arrangements. You will also soon receive a mailing from Dr. Mary Dugan, my internship supervisor at Midwest State University. She will confirm my placement and provide you with additional information about Midwest State's internship program.

Thanks again for offering me an internship position. I am looking forward to learning from you and your excellent staff.

Sincerely,

Jocelyn P. Wells
101 Jenkins Lane
Petersburg, VA 39778
(000) 242-5973

SAMPLE LETTER OF DECLINE #1

                                              143 Hartswick Ave.
                                              Tallahassee, FL 31532
                                              (000) 322-1794

                                              DATE of Typing

Mr. Terrance Brown
Golf Professional
Liberty Golf Club and Resort
Golf Club Lane
Sunnydale, FL 33179

Dear Mr. Brown:

Thank you for your offer of an internship at Liberty Golf Club and Resort. As you know, I was very impressed with your operation, and enjoyed meeting you and your excellent staff.

I am certain that an internship under your supervision would be a valuable learning experience for any student. However, I must decline your generous offer. After careful consideration, I have decided to do my internship at New Venture Country Club in New Orleans. As you know, New Venture is near my home, and offers an internship that meets my academic and career goals as well.

Thank you for your consideration and for the courtesy that you and your staff extended to me. Perhaps we will have the opportunity to work together in the future.

                                              Sincerely,

                                              Jean Broussard

SAMPLE LETTER OF DECLINE #2

DATE of Typing

Mr. Jason George
Park Superintendent
Point Pleasant View Park
Seaview, ME 77490

Dear Mr. George:

I would like to thank you again for interviewing me on March 12, and I sincerely appreciate your willingness to supervise my senior internship. As much as I appreciate your offer, however, I am afraid I must decline at this time.

Although Point Pleasant View Park is an exceptional park, the lack of a full-time naturalist would make it very difficult for me to achieve my internship goals. I have, therefore, decided to accept an internship with Perryville State Park's Nature Center.

Thanks again for offering me an internship position, and please extend my appreciation to your staff for their hospitality during my interview. I thoroughly enjoyed meeting all of you.

Sincerely,

Sujatta Ganesham
900 W. Park Avenue
Midland, TN 48996
(000) 303-9002

Planning for Your Internship

Getting ready for your internship is exciting, but it also involves hard work and thorough planning. This is especially true if you select an internship agency that is distant from your home or school. The following information intends to help you plan for your internship experience.

The Student, Agency, and University Relationship

Your internship is supported by an interdependent relationship among yourself as the student, your university faculty supervisor, and your internship agency supervisor. Each party has defined responsibilities in an effort to facilitate a successful internship experience. It is important for you to speak to your university faculty to gain a better understanding of how the internship paradigm (illustrated below) works within the context of your specific program of study.

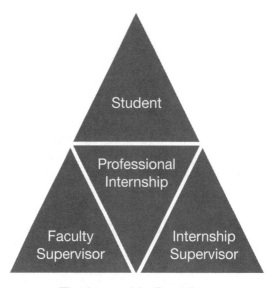

The Internship Paradigm

Communication

It is vital for you to establish and maintain good communication with your agency supervisor and university faculty. Any problems, concerns, or changes in plans need to be clearly communicated to appropriate personnel. Research has demonstrated that communication is the single most important element in a successful internship experience.

Professionalism

For most students, the internship marks their entry into the professional world. You should prepare for your entry by displaying a professional attitude. Your university's courses have laid the groundwork for this attitude (e.g., proper treatment of clients or customers, use of appropriate terminology, dedication to service excellence, cooperation with supervisors and coworkers). Now, your internship offers you the chance to demonstrate responsible behaviors and work habits that epitomize a professional. *Characteristics of a Good Employee* provides attributes you should display on your internship.

Characteristics of a Good Employee

Leader	Observant	Punctual	Good listener
Initiator	Assertive	Clear values	Honest
Motivated	Reliable	Efficient	Friendly
Risk taker	Dynamic	Fair	Adaptable
Knowledgeable	Diligent	Respectful	Displays positive attitude
Communicative	Dependable	Open-minded	Approachable
Problem solver	Resourceful	Foresighted	Manages time well
Accepts criticism	Determined	Organized	Displays sense of humor
Optimistic	Professional	Energetic	Independent
Quick learner	Focused	Intelligent	Patient
Interactive	Tactful	Helpful	Conscientious
Team worker	Ethical	Consistent	Creative
Empathetic	Talented	Practical	Confident
Humble	Attentive	Caring	

Attire

Proper dress depends largely upon the type of agency you select and the nature of your duties. Think back on your interview, visualize the clothing worn by agency staff and interns, and plan to dress accordingly. You should also check with your agency supervisor, in advance, to determine if there are special clothing requirements for interns. For example, some agencies provide uniforms for employees and interns. If you are moving away from school or home, be sure to pack clothing for both work and recreation.

Expenses

Be sure to assess how much it will cost you to live at your internship site and plan your finances carefully. Some agencies, for example, provide free food or housing for interns, but others require that interns pay for everything. Also, transportation costs are sometimes covered by agencies, but generally they are the intern's responsibility.

Resources and References

While in school you have probably accumulated a large amount of materials that will prove helpful during your internship. Select the most important ones and be sure to take them with you. Textbooks, course notes, resource files, and professional journals may be extremely useful to both you and your supervisor. If your internship is away from home or school, remember to take important phone numbers with you, too.

Time Management

Punctuality and promptness are valuable assets for any professional, including interns. A few items are extremely helpful in using your time wisely, including (1) a reliable watch, (2) a good alarm clock, and (3) a schedule book or daily planner. Be sure you have all three while on your internship.

Supplies and Equipment

Be sure to take or have access to supplies and equipment that are important for your internship responsibilities. Depending on your duties or assignments, one or more of the following may prove helpful: calculator, personal computer, recording device, art supplies, drafting tools, and sports equipment.

Orientation

Most agencies have excellent and complete orientation programs, but you still need to do your homework before starting your internship. Prior to arriving for the first day, review promotional materials and all information you have collected about the agency. It may prove embarrassing if you have forgotten some important details about the agency, its services, and its rules and regulations. Moreover, you should take the time to develop a comprehensive list of questions that you want to have answered during your orientation. If the agency's orientation does not cover all of your concerns, you will be ready to ask questions such as the following:

- To whom do I report if my immediate supervisor is not available?
- What is appropriate attire on the job? Are there any aspects of the internship that require other types of attire?
- What are the agency's procedures in case of fire or other emergency situation?
- Do I need keys to any locked areas or doorways? If so, who issues them?
- Does the agency provide liability insurance for interns? If so, am I covered while driving the company's or my own automobile on assigned duties?
- What are the procedures if an employee, guest, or client is injured and needs medical attention?
- Are personal leave days allowed for interns? If so, what are the procedures for requesting a personal leave day?
- If I am sick and unable to work, to whom do I report my illness?
- Are interns notified if the agency will not be open due to severe weather? If not, how can I find out if the agency will be closed?
- What are the names and telephone numbers of coworkers and "key" people in the company? Is there a company directory that is available for interns?
- Are there any policies, procedures, or restrictions that apply to interns on the job? What about during "off duty" time?
- What are the procedures for evaluation of interns? Are there specific forms that are used? If so, would they provide you with a blank form to help guide your behavior during the internship?

Summary

This final chapter was designed to help you select your internship agency. By carefully evaluating your choices, you will be able to select the best possible internship for you. Once this decision is made, you need to communicate your choice in a professional manner, including writing letters to the agency you selected and to the ones you declined. Finally, you should prepare for your internship by thoroughly planning for your needs. By selecting your agency wisely and planning thoroughly, you will assure yourself of a successful internship experience.

Final Comment from Authors

Congratulations on completing this manual. We hope that it has been helpful to you. Although intended primarily as a guide to internships, this manual is also a valuable resource for finding employment in recreation and leisure services. The skills needed to find and apply for an internship are essentially the same as finding and applying for a full-time job. Thus, the information, exercises, and resources in this manual should prove helpful to you as you approach graduation and seek a full-time job in the field. If you have any suggestions to improve this manual or would like to provide information for future updates, please send them to

Edward E. Seagle Jr., EdD
Department of Recreation & Parks Management
California State University, Chico
Chico, CA 95929-0560

Appendix A
Online Resources

This section provides a list of employment-related websites that may help you in your internship search process. Although not listed here, many state recreation and park societies or associations have their own websites with employment information. We suggest checking with the state society or association in your area to see if they maintain a website or have print materials containing internship or job information. You should also check to see if internship-related online or print materials are available from your internship coordinator, other faculty members, or your university's library.

The following online resources are divided into two sections. The first section provides websites that focus upon recreation-related jobs and internships. The second section lists some of the many general career and employment sites available on the Web. Both sections may help you identify internship and employment opportunities, as well as assist in your job search after graduation. All websites in this appendix were active at the time of publication; however, please keep in mind that websites are sometimes removed from the Internet or they may not be accessible because they have changed their location (URL).

Recreation-Related Employment and Internship Sites

Title: Action without Borders/Idealist.org
Address: http://www.idealist.org
Comments: Gives international service-related information. Database of jobs (paid or volunteer) and internships throughout the world; comprehensive list of service-related organizations; resources and newsletters.

Title: American Therapeutic Recreation Association
Address: http://www.atra-online.com
Comments: Provides employment listings in therapeutic recreation. Job listings; career information; professional services and information.

Title: Association for Experiential Education (Jobs Clearinghouse Online)
Address: http://www.aee.org
Comments: Lists jobs and internships emphasizing outdoor recreation and adventure education. Database of full-time, seasonal, and internship positions; national listings by state, plus international opportunities; newsletter; online résumé services.

Title: Casino Careers Online
Address: http://www.casinocareers.com/jobsearch.php
Comments: Offers information on jobs at casinos and related businesses nationwide. Database of full-time and seasonal positions; résumé services; career guides and resources.

Title: Club Managers Association of America Internships: Club Careers
Address: http://www.clubcareers.org/
Comments: Provides information on club management internships nationally. Database of internships; résumé and cover letter assistance; résumé bank. Entrance to certain areas requires paid membership.

Title: Coolworks.com
Address: http://www.coolworks.com
Comments: Offers a variety of information and services emphasizing commercial recreation and outdoor recreation. Database of seasonal positions and internships; online résumé service; automated job and internship searches.

Title: Cross-Cultural Solutions
Address: CrossCulturalSolutions.org
Comments: Information on international internships and volunteer experiences. Related links.

Title: Cyber-Sierra's Natural Resources Job Search
Address: http://www.cyber-sierra.com/nrjobs/index.html
Comments: Emphasizes employment and internship opportunities related to natural resources and conservation. Database with jobs and internships by category; career-related tools and resources.

Title: EcoEmploy.com
Address: EcoEmploy.com
Comments: Environment-related employment in the U.S. and Canada. Emphasis on natural and green positions.

Title: Environmental Career Center
Address: http://environmentalcareer.com/job-board
Comments: Provides employment and internship opportunities related to the environment. Database with jobs and internships.

Title: ECO.org
Address: http://www.eco.org
Comments: Emphasizes paid opportunities related to the environment.

Title: GoAbroad.com
Address: http://www.goabroad.com/intern-abroad
Comments: Offers comprehensive information for international study and travel. International internship database; search capacity by country and type of internship, including recreation-related categories.

Title: Hospitality Careers Online
Address: http://www.hcareers.com
Comments: Provides employment listings in hospitality and related industries. Database of positions with search capacity; information on job search process.

Title: HealthClubs.com
Address: http://healthclubs.com/job-seeker-resources
Comments: Offers employment information related to health and fitness clubs nationally and internationally. Database with employment listings by state/country; industry information; career assistance and resources.

Title: Hospitality Jobs Online
Address: http://www.hospitalityonline.com/
Comments: Enables search for job opportunities in hospitality and related industries. Database search by job category.

Title: Hotel Jobs Network
Address: http://www.hoteljobsnetwork.com/
Comments: Provides employer information and hourly/student employment opportunities in hotel services nationwide.

Title: Indiana State University's Recreation Internship (Practicum) Sites
Address: http://www.indstate.edu/krs/students/students.htm
Comments: Lists internship sites affiliated with ISU's Department of Kinesiology Recreation, and Sport.

Title: International Association of Amusement Parks and Attractions
Address: http://www.iaapa.org/
Comments: Provides employment and internship opportunities in amusement parks and related industries. Database with career opportunities, including internships.

Title: International Festivals and Event Association
Address: http://www.ifea.com/resources/re_pg_1.htm
Comments: Offers employment information related to festivals and events. Job bank with jobs and internships.

Title: National Association of Development Organizations Job Opportunities
Address: http://www.nado.org/jobs/
Comments: Lists jobs across the country in regional development, with emphasis upon small metropolitan and rural areas.

Title: National Intramural–Recreational Sports Association's Bluefishjobs.com
Address: http://www.bluefishjobs.com
Comments: Provides information on jobs in intramural sports and recreation-related agencies. Database of vacancies nationally; personal accounts and résumé services; jobseeker help.

Title: National Recreation and Park Association Career Center
Address: http://careercenter.nrpa.org/index.cfm?
Comments: Lists recreation-related jobs and internships throughout the country; résumé posting; membership required for full access.

Title: National Wildlife Federation
Address: http://www.nwf.org/About/jobs-at-MWF.aspx
Comments: Lists employment and internship opportunities offered by the National Wildlife Federation.

Title: Recreation Internships
Address: http://schlags.com/paul/internships
Comments: Database listing recreation-related internships. Also provides job listings.

Title: Recreation Resources Service (North Carolina State University)
Address: http://cnr.ncsu.edu/rrs/jobs.php
Comments: Provides listing of in-state and national job opportunities. Additional resources; links to local, regional, and national employment sites.

Title: Resort Intern Connection
Address: http://www.resortinternconnection.com
Comments: Provides information on internships in resorts located in Hilton Head Island and Myrtle Beach, South Carolina.

Title: ResortJobs.com
Address: http://www.resortjobs.com
Comments: Presents information on jobs at national and international resorts, as well as other recreation-related businesses. Database of employment opportunities; keyword or location search capacity; job-related tools and tips.

Title: Simply Hired
Address: Simplyhired.com
Comments: Lists internships with keyword and location search capacity

Title: Student Conservation Association's Volunteer, Internship, and Employment Opportunities
Address: http://www.thesca.or
Comments: Lists volunteer, internship, and employment opportunities related to the environment.

Title: Therapeutic Recreation Directory
Address: http://www.recreationtherapy.com/rt.htm
Comments: Provides a variety of information and resources on therapeutic recreation. Job listings and internship postings; career-related resources; links to other recreation-related sites.

Title: University of North Dakota Internship Search Resources
Address: http://www.und.nodak.edu/dept/rls/intern/finder1.htm
Comments: Lists internship sites affiliated with the university, plus links to a variety of recreation-related internship resources.

General Career, Employment, and Internship Sites

Title: AfterCollege
Address: http://www.jobresource.com
Comments: Features employment and internship database, plus other career information. Free registration; résumé services; career assistance.

Title: Black Collegian Online
Address: http://www.blackcollegian.com
Comments: Provides extensive job-related services and information for African-American job seekers. Database with search options; employer profiles; feature articles; online career service.

Title: CareerJournal
Address: http://online.wsj.com/careers
Comments: *Wall Street Journal* site provides the day's top job-related stories and includes Job Hunting Tips and Find a Job feature. Also provides links to an extensive list of high-quality articles, databases, and other employment-related services.

Title: Careermag.com
Address: http://www.careermag.com
Comments: Offers extensive job-related services and information. Automated search capacity; online résumé posting; reference materials and articles.

Title: Career One Stop
Address: http://www.careeronestop.org
Comments: Includes comprehensive job-related services and information. Database with jobs nationally; online résumé and interview service; career-related help line.

Title: CareerSite.com
Address: http://400.careersite.com
Comments: Provides comprehensive database of job listings by state. Keyword search capacity; online résumé posting; company profiles; career tools.

Title: CollegeGrad.com
Address: http://www.collegegrad.com
Comments: Includes internship and entry-level employment database, plus employment services and information. Career planning and job-seeking information; résumé services; social media links.

Title: College News
Address: http://www.collegenews.com
Comments: Limited career resources, with links to other employment sites; useful information on all aspects of college life.

Title: Internet Career Connection
Address: http://www.iccweb.com
Comments: Comprehensive career services and information. Step-by-step career planning; advice on searching for jobs.

Title: Internet Job Source
Address: http://www.50statejobs.com
Comments: Job search by state and category. Keyword search capacity; job-related links.

Title: InternJobs.com
Address: http://internjobs.com
Comments: Provides comprehensive job and internship information. Database of internships nationally; keyword or location search capacity; partner site with AboutJobs.com.

Title: InternshipPrograms.com
Address: http://www.internshipprograms.com/
Comments: An internship search engine. Allows students to post résumés and search an internship database, with some opportunities in recreation-related organizations. Registration required.

Title: Job Source Network
Address: http://www.jobsourcenetwork.com
Comments: Provides links to comprehensive career services and information.

Title: Job-Hunt.org
Address: http://www.job-hunt.org
Comments: Offers comprehensive career-related services and information. Database of job listings; online résumé service; career tools; reference materials and articles; links to other career sites.

Title: Job-interview.net
Address: http://www.job-interview.net
Comments: Offers an extensive collection of interview-related information, including interview questions, tips for interviewees, and suggestions to prepare for an interview.

Title: JobWeb.com
Address: http://www.jobweb.com
Comments: Excellent collection of articles and advice for students seeking jobs and internships. Features include interview tips and how to market yourself.

Title: Monster.com
Address: http://www.monster.com
Comments: Provides extensive job-related services and information; national and international job listings; online résumé service; automated job search; reference materials.

Title: Quintessential Careers
Address: http://www.quintcareers.com
Comments: Offers comprehensive job-related services and information. Reference materials and articles; career tool kit; searchable database; résumé service; free online newsletter.

Title: USA Jobs
Address: http://www.usajobs.opm.gov
Comments: Focuses on federal employment opportunities. Searchable database of government jobs; online applications; resources and résumé help.

Title: USInterns.com
Address: http://www.usinterns.com
Comments: Provides links to searchable database with thousands of internship opportunities.

Title: Yahoo! Careers
Address: http://careers.yahoo.com
Comments: Database of internship and job listings. Keyword job search capacity.

Appendix B
National Associations and Organizations

The following list includes national organizations related to recreation and leisure services. Student memberships are often available at reduced rates and internship (and employment) information is sometimes available at little or no extra charge. You should contact the organizations that interest you to determine what services they provide to student members.

For information on additional national and international organizations, we suggest you consult the *Encyclopedia of Associations,* an annual publication of Gale Cengage Learning Company, Detroit, MI. This publication is available in the reference section of most university libraries.

Aerobics and Fitness Association of America
15250 Ventura Boulevard, Suite 200
Sherman Oaks, CA 91403
(877) 968-7263
http://www.afaa.com

American Alliance of Health, Physical Education,
Recreation and Dance (AAHPERD)
1900 Association Drive
Reston, VA 22091
(800) 213-7193
http://www.aahperd.org

American Association of Museums
1575 Eye Street Northwest, Suite 400
Washington, DC 20005
(202) 289-1818
http://www.aam-us.org

American Camping Association
5000 State Road 67 North
Martinsville, IN 46151-7902
(765) 342-8456
http://www.acacamps.org

American Therapeutic Recreation Association
629 North Main Street
Hattiesburg, MS 39401
(601) 450-ATRA
http://www.atra-online.com

Aquatic Exercise Association
201 S. Tamiami Trail, Suite 3
Nokomis, FL 34275
(941) 486-8600 or (888) AEA-WAVE
http://www.aeawave.com

Association for Experiential Education
3775 Iris Avenue, Suite #4
Boulder, CO 80301
(303) 440-8844
http://www.aee.org

Club Managers Association of America
1733 King Street
Alexandria, VA 22314
(703) 739-9500
http://www.cmaa.org

Employee Morale and Recreation Association
P.O. Box 10517
Rockville, MD 20849
E-mail: esmahq@esmassn.org
http://www.esmassn.org

International Association of Amusement Parks and Attractions (IAAPA)
1448 Duke Street
Alexandria, VA 22314
(703) 836-4800
http://www.iaapa.org

IDEA Health and Fitness Association
10455 Pacific Center Court
San Diego, CA 92121
(800) 999-4332, ext. 7
http://www.ideafit.com

International Festivals and Events Association
2603 W. Eastover Terrace
Boise, ID 83706
(208) 433-0950
http://www.ifea.com

International Health, Racquet, and Sportsclub Association (IHRSA)
70 Fargo Street
Boston, MA 02210
(800) 228-4772 or (617) 951-0055
http://www.ihrsa.org

National Club Association
1201 15th Street NW, Suite 450
Washington, DC 20005
(202) 822-9822
http://www.natlclub.org

National Council for Therapeutic Recreation Certification (NCTRC)
7 Elmwood Drive
New City, NY 10956
(845) 639-1439
http://www.nctrc.org
Note: NCTRC is a certifying organization.

National Intramural–Recreational Sports Association
4185 SW Research Way
Corvallis, OR 97333
(541) 766-8211
http://www.nirsa.org/home.htm

National Recreation and Park Association
22377 Belmont Ridge Road
Ashburn, VA 20148
(800) 626-NRPA
http://www.nrpa.org

National Strength and Conditioning Association
1885 Bob Johnson Drive
Colorado Springs, CO 80906
(719) 632-6722
http://www.nsca-lift.org

National Wildlife Federation
11100 Wildlife Center Drive
Reston, VA 20190
(703) 438-6000
http://www.nwf.org

Student Conservation Association, Inc.
P.O. Box 550
Charlestown, NH 03603
(603) 543-1700
http://www.sca-inc.org

Appendix C
Recommended Readings

Allen, J. G. (2004). *The complete Q & A job interview book*. New York: John Wiley & Sons.

Berger, L. (2012). *All Work, No Pay: Finding an Internship, Building Your Résumé, Making Connections, and Gaining Job Experience*. Berkeley, CA: Ten Speed Press.

Beshara, T. (2006). *The job search solution: The ultimate system for finding a great job now!* New York: AMACOM.

Betrus, M. (2005). *Perfect phrases for cover letters*. New York: McGraw-Hill.

Block, J., & Betrus, M. (2004). *Great answers! Great questions! For your job interview*. New York: McGraw-Hill.

Bloomberg, G., & Holden, M. (1999). *The women's job search handbook*. Charlotte, VT: Williamson.

Bolles, M. E., & Bolles, R. N. (2008). *Job hunting online*. Berkeley, CA: Ten Speed Press.

Bolles, R. N. (2010). *What color is your parachute?: A practical manual for job-hunters and career-changer?* Berkeley, CA: Ten Speed Press.

Bright, J., & Earl, J. (2006). *Amazing résumés: What employers want to see—and how to say it*. Indianapolis, IN: JIST Works.

Carter, C. (2004). *Majoring in the rest of your life: Career secrets for college students*. New York: The Noonday Press.

Coplin, W. D. (2003). *10 things employers want you to learn in college: The know-how you need to succeed*. Berkeley, CA: Ten Speed Press.

DeLuca, M. (2010). *Best answers to the 201 most frequently asked interview questions*. New York: McGraw-Hill.

Dickel, M. R., & Roehm, F. E. (2008). *The guide to Internet job searching*. New York: McGraw-Hill.

Dison, P. (2000). *Job searching online for dummies*. Indianapolis, IN: IDG Books Worldwide.

Donovan, C. P., & Garnett, J. (2001). *Internships for dummies*. New York: Hungry Minds.

Enelow, W., & Boldt, A. (2006). *No-nonsense cover letters: The essential guide to creating attention-grabbing cover letters that get interviews & job offers*. Franklin Lakes, NJ: Career Press.

Epstein, L., Korten, A., & Wu, P. (2007). *You're hired! Interview skills to get the job*. Arlington, VA: E3 Publishing.

Farr, J. M. (2007). *Getting the job you really want: A step-by-step guide to finding a good job in less time*. Indianapolis, IN: JIST Publishing.

Filho, W. L. (Ed.). (2001). *Environmental careers, environmental employment and environmental training: International approaches and contexts*. New York: Peter Lang.

Fox, J. (2007). *How to land your dream job: No résumé! And other secrets to get you in the door*. New York: Hyperion.

Greene, B. (2004). *Get the interview every time: Proven résumé and cover letter strategies from Fortune 500 hiring professionals*. New York: Kaplan.

Hachey, J. (2007). *The big guide to living and working overseas: 3,045 career building resource*. Toronto, Ontario, Canada: Intercultural Systems.

Kador, J. (2002). *201 best questions to ask on your interview*. New York: McGraw-Hill.

Kennedy, J. L. (2007). *Résumés for dummies*. Hoboken, NJ: Wiley.

Kessler, R. (2006). *Competency-based interviews: Master the tough new interview style and give them the answers that will win you the job*. Franklin Lakes, NJ: Career Press.

Kessler, R., & Strasburg, L. A. (2005). *Competency-based résumé: How to bring your résumé to the top of the pile.* Franklin Lakes, NJ: Career Press.

Krannich, R. L., & Krannich, C. R. (2007). *No one will hire me!: Avoid 17 mistakes and win the job.* Manassas Park, VA: Impact.

Landes, M. (2005). *The back door guide to short-term adventures: Internships, extraordinary experiences, seasonal jobs, volunteering, work abroad.* Berkeley, CA: Ten Speed Press.

Levinson, J., & Perry, D. (2005). *Guerrilla marketing for job hunters 3.0: How to stand out from the crowd and tap into the hidden job market using social media and 999 other tactics today.* Hoboken, NJ: Wiley.

Medley, H. A. (2005). *Sweaty palms: The neglected art of being interviewed.* New York: Time Warner.

Nobel, D. F. (2007). *Gallery of best résumés: A collection of quality résumés by professional résumé writers.* Indianapolis, IN: JIST Publishing.

Oliver, V. (2005). *301 Smart answers to tough interview questions.* Naperville, IL: Sourcebooks.

Rosenberg, A. D., & Hizer, D. V. (2007). *The résumé handbook: How to write outstanding résumés and cover letters for every situation.* Avon, MA: Adams Media.

Ryan, D. J. (2004). *Job search handbook for people with disabilities: A complete career planning and job search guide.* Indianapolis, IN: JIST Publishing.

Satterthwaite, F., & D'Orsi, G. (2003). *The career portfolio workbook.* New York: McGraw-Hill.

Taylor, J., & Hardy, D. (2005). *Monster careers: Interviewing: Master the moment that gets you the job.* New York: Penguin Group.

Van Devender, J., & Van Devender-Graves, G. (2007). *Savvy interviewing: How to ace the interview & get the job.* Herndon, VA: Capital Books.

Waldman, J. (2011). *Job searching with social media for dummies.* Hoboken, NJ: Wiley.

Wallace, R. (2006). *Adams cover letter almanac.* Avon, MA: Adams Media.

Walsh, R. (2007). *The complete job search book for college students: A step-by-step guide to finding the right job.* Avon, MA: Adams Media.

Whitcomb, S. (2007). *Résumé magic: Trade secrets of a professional résumé writer.* Indianapolis, IN: JIST Works.

Wise, C. C. (2008). *The vault guide to top internships.* New York: Vault.

Yate, M. J. (Updated Annually). *Knock 'em dead with great answers to tough interview questions.* Avon, MA: Adams Media.

Yate, M. J. (2012). *Knock 'em dead cover letters.* Avon, MA: Adams Media.

Yate, M. J. (2012). *Knock 'em dead résumés.* Avon, MA: Adams Media.

Other books from Venture Publishing, Inc.

21st Century Leisure: Current Issues, Second Edition
by Valeria J. Freysinger and John R. Kelly

Active Living in Older Adulthood: Principles and Practices of Activity Programs
by Barbara A. Hawkins

Activity Experiences and Programming within Long-Term Care
by Ted Tedrick and Elaine R. Green

Adventure Programming
edited by John C. Miles and Simon Priest

Assessment: The Cornerstone of Activity Programs
by Ruth Perschbacher

Beyond Baskets and Beads: Activities for Older Adults with Functional Impairments
by Mary Hart, Karen Primm, and Kathy Cranisky

Boredom Busters: Themed Special Events to Dazzle and Delight Your Group
by Annette C. Moore

Brain Fitness
by Suzanne Fitzsimmons

Client Assessment in Therapeutic Recreation Services
by Norma J. Stumbo

Client Outcomes in Therapeutic Recreation Services
by Norma J. Stumbo

Conceptual Foundations for Therapeutic Recreation
edited by David R. Austin, John Dattilo, and Bryan P. McCormick

Constraints to Leisure
edited by Edgar L. Jackson

Dementia Care Programming: An Identity-Focused Approach
by Rosemary Dunne

Dimensions of Choice: Qualitative Approaches to Parks, Recreation, Tourism, Sport, and Leisure Research, Second Edition
by Karla A. Henderson

Diversity and the Recreation Profession: Organizational Perspectives, Revised Edition
edited by Maria T. Allison and Ingrid E. Schneider

Effective Management in Therapeutic Recreation Service, Second Edition
by Marcia Jean Carter and Gerald S. O'Morrow

Evaluating Leisure Services: Making Enlightened Decisions, Third Edition
by Karla A. Henderson and M. Deborah Bialeschki

Everything from A to Y: The Zest Is up to You! Older Adult Activities for Every Day of the Year
by Nancy R. Cheshire and Martha L. Kenney

Experience Marketing: Strategies for the New Millennium
by Ellen L. O'Sullivan and Kathy J. Spangler

Facilitation of Therapeutic Recreation Services: An Evidence-Based and
Best Practice Approach to Techniques and Processes
   edited by Norma J. Stumbo and Brad Wardlaw

Facilitation Techniques in Therapeutic Recreation, Second Edition
   by John Dattilo and Alexis McKenney

File o' Fun: A Recreation Planner for Games & Activities, Third Edition
   by Jane Harris Ericson and Diane Ruth Albright

Getting People Involved in Life and Activities: Effective Motivating Techniques
   by Jeanne Adams

Health Promotion for Mind, Body, and Spirit
   by Suzanne Fitzsimmons and Linda L. Buettner

Human Resource Management in Recreation, Sport, and Leisure Services
   by Margaret Arnold, Regina Glover, and Cheryl Beeler

Inclusion: Including People With Disabilities in Parks and Recreation Opportunities
   by Lynn Anderson and Carla Brown Kress

Inclusive Leisure Services, Third Edition
   by John Dattilo

Internships in Recreation and Leisure Services: A Practical Guide for Students, Fifth Edition
   by Edward E. Seagle, Jr., Ralph W. Smith, and Tammy B. Smith

Interpretation of Cultural and Natural Resources, Second Edition
   by Douglas M. Knudson, Ted T. Cable, and Larry Beck

Intervention Activities for At-Risk Youth
   by Norma J. Stumbo

Introduction to Outdoor Recreation: Providing and Managing Resource Based Opportunities
   by Roger L. Moore and B.L. Driver

Introduction to Recreation and Leisure Services, Eighth Edition
   by Karla A. Henderson, M. Deborah Bialeschki, John L. Hemingway, Jan S. Hodges, Beth D. Kivel, and H. Douglas Sessoms

Introduction to Therapeutic Recreation: U.S. and Canadian Perspectives
   by Kenneth Mobily and Lisa Ostiguy

An Introduction to Tourism
   by Robert W. Wyllie

Introduction to Writing Goals and Objectives: A Manual for Recreation Therapy Students
and Entry-Level Professionals
   by Suzanne Melcher

Leadership and Administration of Outdoor Pursuits, Third Edition
   by James Blanchard, Michael Strong, and Phyllis Ford

Leadership in Leisure Services: Making a Difference, Third Edition
   by Debra J. Jordan

Leisure and Leisure Services in the 21st Century: Toward Mid Century
   by Geoffrey Godbey

The Leisure Diagnostic Battery Computer Software (CD)
   by Peter A. Witt, Gary Ellis, and Mark A. Widmer

Leisure Education I: A Manual of Activities and Resources, Second Edition
by Norma J. Stumbo

Leisure Education II: More Activities and Resources, Second Edition
by Norma J. Stumbo

Leisure Education III: More Goal-Oriented Activities
by Norma J. Stumbo

Leisure Education IV: Activities for Individuals with Substance Addictions
by Norma J. Stumbo

Leisure Education Program Planning: A Systematic Approach, Third Edition
by John Dattilo

Leisure for Canadians
edited by Ron McCarville and Kelly MacKay

Leisure, Health, and Wellness: Making the Connections
edited by Laura Payne, Barbara Ainsworth, and Geoffrey Godbey

Leisure Studies: Prospects for the Twenty-First Century
edited by Edgar L. Jackson and Thomas L. Burton

Leisure in Your Life: New Perspectives
by Geoffrey Godbey

Making a Difference in Academic Life: A Handbook for Park, Recreation, and Tourism Educators
and Graduate Students
edited by Dan Dustin and Tom Goodale

Managing to Optimize the Beneficial Outcomes of Leisure
edited by B. L. Driver

Marketing in Leisure and Tourism: Reaching New Heights
by Patricia Click Janes

More Than a Game: A New Focus on Senior Activity Services
by Brenda Corbett

The Multiple Values of Wilderness
by H. Ken Cordell, John C. Bergstrom, and J. M. Bowker

N.E.S.T. Approach: Dementia Practice Guidelines for Disturbing Behaviors
by Linda L. Buettner and Suzanne Fitzsimmons

The Organizational Basis of Leisure Participation: A Motivational Exploration
by Robert A. Stebbins

Outdoor Recreation for 21st Century America
by H. Ken Cordell

Parks for Life: Moving the Goal Posts, Changing the Rules, and Expanding the Field
by Will LaPage

The Pivotal Role of Leisure Education: Finding Personal Fulfillment in This Century
edited by Elie Cohen-Gewerc and Robert A. Stebbins

Planning and Organizing Group Activities in Social Recreation
by John V. Valentine

Planning Areas and Facilities for Sport and Recreation: Predesign Process, Principles, and Strategies
by Jack A. Harper

Planning Parks for People, Second Edition
  by John Hultsman, Richard L. Cottrell, and Wendy Z. Hultsman

Programming for Parks, Recreation, and Leisure Services: A Servant Leadership Approach, Third Edition
  by Donald G. DeGraaf, Debra J. Jordan, and Kathy H. DeGraaf

Puttin' on the Skits: Plays for Adults in Managed Care
  by Jean Vetter

Recreation and Leisure: Issues in an Era of Change, Third Edition
  edited by Thomas Goodale and Peter A. Witt

Recreation and Youth Development
  by Peter A. Witt and Linda L. Caldwell

Recreation for Older Adults: Individual and Group Activities
  by Judith A. Elliott and Jerold E. Elliott

Recreation Program Planning Manual for Older Adults
  by Karen Kindrachuk

Recreation Programming and Activities for Older Adults
  by Jerold E. Elliott and Judith A. Sorg-Elliott

Reference Manual for Writing Rehabilitation Therapy Treatment Plans
  by Penny Hogberg and Mary Johnson

Service Living: Building Community through Public Parks and Recreation
  by Doug Wellman, Dan Dustin, Karla Henderson, and Roger Moore

Simple Expressions: Creative and Therapeutic Arts for the Elderly in Long-Term Care Facilities
  by Vicki Parsons

A Social Psychology of Leisure, Second Edition
  by Douglas A. Kleiber, Gordon J. Walker, and Roger C. Mannell

Special Events and Festivals: How to Organize, Plan, and Implement
  by Angie Prosser and Ashli Rutledge

The Sportsman's Voice: Hunting and Fishing in America
  by Mark Damian Duda, Martin F. Jones, and Andrea Criscione

Survey Research and Analysis: Applications in Parks, Recreation, and Human Dimensions
  by Jerry Vaske

Taking the Initiative: Activities to Enhance Effectiveness and Promote Fun
  by J. P. Witman

Therapeutic Recreation and the Nature of Disabilities
  by Kenneth E. Mobily and Richard D. MacNeil

Therapeutic Recreation: Cases and Exercises, Second Edition
  by Barbara C. Wilhite and M. Jean Keller

Therapeutic Recreation in Health Promotion and Rehabilitation
  by John Shank and Catherine Coyle

Therapeutic Recreation in the Nursing Home
  by Linda Buettner and Shelley L. Martin

Therapeutic Recreation Programming: Theory and Practice
  by Charles Sylvester, Judith E. Voelkl, and Gary D. Ellis

Rec
may 2013 **Date Due**

OCT 1 0 2013 @ WC			

BRODART, CO.   Cat. No. 23-233   Printed in U.S.A.